£3.25

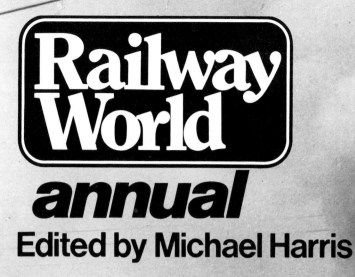

Railway World
annual
1980

Edited by Michael Harris

LONDON
IAN ALLAN LTD

Contents

First published 1979

ISBN 0 7110 0933 3

Published by Ian Allan Ltd, Shepperton, Surrey; and printed in the United Kingdom by Ian Allan Printing Ltd

Cover: BR Standard '9F' 2-10-0 No 92220 *Evening Star* at Ais Gill summit with a charter train special on 13 May 1978. / *W. A. Sharman*

Front endpaper: A powerful example of 'diesel appeal' as Class 45 diesel No 45.049 sweeps round the curve at the approach to Wellingborough from the north with a loaded tanker train on 4 March 1976. / *Philip D. Hawkins*

Title page: A murky, chilly morning at York as 'A1' Pacific No 60119 *Patrick Stirling* steams through the mist with the 10.00 semi-fast to Edinburgh, past a 'K1' 2-6-0, on 18 January 1964. / *M. Dunnett*

This picture: Peckett 0-6-0ST (No 1426 of 1916) shunts at Brynlliw Colliery on the afternoon of 18 September 1974. / *David Eatwell*

A personal Paddington

MICHAEL HARRIS

From time to time the national and London evening newspapers have 'discovered' Paddington and certainly the station has always had a pretty good press. More recently there has been good reason, with the station's 125th anniversary, the unveiling of a statue to Paddington Bear and the famous 14 pound cat in the station's Ladies. Paddington has all the makings of becoming a public institution, bolstered by its appearance in fiction such as Agatha Christie's *4.50 from Paddington* or John Wain's compelling and poignant *The Smaller Sky*. Unlike other London termini such as Liverpool Street, St Pancras or Waterloo, Paddington has a compactness, a human dimension which makes it one of the most successful public buildings we have. The most concise and feeling cameo I know is Ian Nairn's in *Nairn's London* (Penguin Books 1966) and he summarises by saying that 'the result has to be taken down all at once and can't be broken down into constituents'.

And this is where the railway enthusiast comes in. To us the station is essentially a collection of general impressions, peopled by locomotives, trains and atmosphere. Strangely, the station's atmosphere has not changed with dieselisation. The sound of the high-revving engines of the 'Warships', 'Hymeks' or 'Westerns' filled Paddington's air space as well as that of the IC125s' Valentas does now. Modernisation generally has served to improve the detail, from the 1960s paint scheme to the high power lighting, while many of the less happy efforts have been shrugged off with impunity. Recent improvements have meant a successful tidying up but, curiously, nothing has been done to give the station a satisfactory, inexpensive restaurant — a refinement it has long wanted. Retreating to the Great Western Royal Hotel really misses the point.

But what was that general atmosphere earlier alluded to? To me it was the Paddington of the late 1950s on a cold winter afternoon. From the end of Platform 8 an empty stock train can be seen approaching, dropping down to stop at the signals alongside the parcels platform. The '57xx' simmers, its headlamps shining. Getting the road, the pannier tank makes a noisy show as it brings its coaches up to the

Above: Paddington station on the second day of 1961. An NBL B-B diesel hydraulic has just brought in an up express and a dmu is in the background. The station is in its old colour scheme and with less powerful lighting. / *British Rail*

3

outer platform ends. In due course, a 'King' or 'Castle' slides down from Ranelagh Bridge and backs quietly into the station. Later 'RA' will show up on the indicator by the bridge and, having sat for the last 10-15 minutes on its train, a steady, efficient Paddington start will be made. Strange what individual noises GWR engines could make, but none so individual as the double-chimneyed 'Kings' and 'Castles', the former being capable of a bass humming, often intermittent, as if the locomotive was having a quiet doze before making a start for Wolverhampton or Plymouth.

But, of course, it was different in summer and the number of locomotive and train movements was often extraordinary. It's tempting to think that all ran perfectly, but this is wrong. On a summer Saturday the old GWR arrivals indicator on the Lawn would often show all trains as running 99 minutes late; not a triumph of exactitude but revealing the fact that the trains involved were over 100 minutes late and the indicator, reasonably enough, had two tracks only for each arrivals column. There were the queues, also, although 10 years earlier they would have strung out from the station along Eastbourne Terrace.

There were other specialities, too. Whenever there was a special occasion, out came the station officials' GWR pillbox hats, and as George Behrend has previously remarked, there was the GWR staff band with the 'G' on the collecting box somewhat obviously painted out. But surprises have come more recently than that. Arriving late at night in the terminus during the 1967/8 resignalling, I was astounded to see a complete train of Great Western coaches at Platform 10 or 11. Toplights and bow enders were all there but these were engineers' coaches. More recently, the illusion has been reality when a complete train of restored GWR coaches has appeared.

Some of the more unusual trains using Paddington have received their due attention from other writers such as the 14.35 to Bristol via Devizes, but there were other curiosities like the 15.18 to Wolverhampton calling at Ealing Broadway, Slough, Maidenhead, Twyford, Reading and almost all stations to Oxford, taking 146 minutes to cover the first 63 miles. There was also the Thame-Paddington midday train and the 16.34 'shoppers' special' from Paddington-Banbury

Left: The station has now been repainted in its current scheme in this 23 April 1965 view which features *Clun Castle* at the head of the 16.10 to Bicester (the 'shoppers' special'). A 'Western' has brought in the empty stock. / *Carl Symes*

Below left: Bearing a target number, condensing pannier tank No 9707 brings empty stock for Paddington past Subway Junction box (east of Westbourne Park) on 18 April 1960. / *Michael H. C. Baker*

Below: A view from the Paddington departure platforms. 'The Bristol Pullman' approaches Platform 4 as empty stock, a steam-hauled express leaves Platform 2 and '94xx' 0-6-0PT No 8459 takes empty coaches away from Platform 10. A September 1961 view. / *B. H. Jackson*

which picked up the Bicester slip coach later in its journey. By the late 1950s trains such as this were of interest to the enthusiast as they were still made up of GWR coaches, already displaced on principal services out of Paddington by BR standard stock.

The winter 1959 timetables saw the end of quite a chunk of Great Western atmosphere with the dieselisation of some of the semi-fast trains such as the 16.00 Paddington-Swindon and Oxford-Didcot-Paddington services worked by 'Halls'. Before long, the Pressed Steel three-car dmus had arrived to dieselise the Paddington suburban trains — not before time when it came to economic operation. Nonetheless, the '61xx' 2-6-2Ts handled the suburban trains with great style, their characteristic, apart from the 'burping noises' and enthusiastic starts, being the whistling sound as they ran up to the suburban platform ends with regulators closed.

Into the early 1960s, despite dieselisation and tidying up of the weekday trains, the Sunday service retained some odd survivals. The old pattern of trains was not greatly altered and, possibly as a result, different train sets were used, primarily made up of GWR coaches. So the connoisseur of such vehicles could often spot some rare birds which were to last until the purges of old stock in 1962/3. Reverting to the suburban services, the steam sets had some interesting formations, and although the majority were of five coaches (two second brakes, two seconds and a composite), a few were made up to eight including a solitary corridor composite. Some of the peak hour trains, such as the 17.20/17.35 to Didcot and 18.15 Henley, retained the same formations for months or years, the corridor sets getting an outing on summer Saturday holiday trains. Another peculiarity was the Sunday 15.33 from Paddington, nominally one of the semi-fast local Reading trains but actually going on to Swindon, formed of corridor stock hauled by a 'Castle' or 'County'. At one time near the top of the league of BR's fastest trains, the 17.35 non-stop from Oxford to Paddington in 60min was a strange service. Later, it came up from Worcester calling at almost all stations to Oxford, but in 1959 was a real 'Worse and Worse' (Oxford, Worcester and Wolverhampton) line train, originating from Wolverhampton at 14.15 and travelling via Stourbridge Junction and Kidderminster to Worcester. At Oxford the train was usually made up to six coaches, and like other secondary trains (despite its 63.4mile/h booking to Paddington) it was normally a formation of GWR stock.

To return to the main line, I find it intriguing to look at my notebooks of the late 1950s/early 1960s for they reveal a pattern and detail of train operation which is as far removed from today as the timetables of the 1930s. Certainly, the cost of operating the railway in the same manner as then would be prohibitive and it is not surprising that the WR managers of the mid-1960s reckoned they had to move fast to prevent the region descending like a stone into the well of bankruptcy. Even so, the old scene was a lot of fun to watch.

Paddington on Christmas Eve 1959 gives some clue to operations at the start of the transition to diesel traction, on a day when relief trains were being run to get people away for their holidays. The empty stock pilots were mainly '94xx' 0-6-0PTs, helped out by '15xxs' and '97xx' condensing panniers, further assisted by locomotives being worked down from Old Oak on empty stock before heading out on main line trains. Between 10.00 and 14.00, despite seven reliefs and one train running in two parts, punctuality for down departures was good. Forty-two trains in four hours was not bad going seeing that before resignalling main line trains were not generally turned round in the station, apart from Worcester services. The 10.05 Weston had a 'County', No 1010, but motive power on other expresses was much as expected, except that the 12.45 Worcester had 'Hall' No 4961, the 12.47 Bristol relief had 'King' No 6021 and the 12.55 Swansea relief featured Canton 'Britannia' No 70027. By this date diesel traction was in command of West of England trains: the 'Cornish Riviera' had D801, the 'Torbay', D803, and the 'Mayflower', D804. Even so, the West Country reliefs were all steam powered. Diesel units had already been introduced on the 18 minutes past semi-fasts (such as the 10.18/11.18), but the 12.18 Oxford's five compartment coaches were graced by Reading's 'Castle' No 5018, the 13.18 Oxford had a '61xx' and a 12.15 Newbury relief was run (an eight-coach suburban set with corridor composite) headed by 'Grange' No 6854.

As to the reliefs, these were predictable by those days' standards, being the usual division of a principal service such as the 'Cornish Riviera' or South Wales expresses (some like the 11.35 and 13.50 being bound for the now defunct Neyland), but an 11.00 Wrexham relief was more surprising. In the main, train reporting numbers were carried by the locomotives but pressure at Ranelagh Bridge or Old Oak was suggested by their absence on later trains. By the end of the lunch-hour, some heavier loads were being taken, Cheltenham, of all places, having a 14-coach train on the 13.40 (this train usually being a Weston and Cheltenham combined service) which left several minutes late in the charge of 'Castle' No 5094. A less happy result might have been expected on the 13.55 Pembroke Dock relief on which 'Hall' No 5997 was saddled with 13 bogies; by contrast the 12.30 Weymouth with nine on had two 'Halls' familiar to the Paddington scene, Nos 5936/6910.

There were no great surprises on the rolling stock side, one of the 1937-40 Excursion sets, based at

Craven Arms, being used for the previously mentioned Wrexham relief. A few early Collett 70ft coaches put in an appearance on relief trains, and one of the nondescript saloon brakes, No 9109, similarly, but otherwise the observer would have been treated to the pleasing sight of all types of 1923-48 standard GWR stock.

Easter 1961 (30 March, to be precise) gave much the same general picture, but now the suburban trains were dmu-worked. This was a day when the Bristol and Birmingham Pullmans were running but the number of down reliefs, just between 10.05 and 16.25, was quite an eye-opener by today's standards given, however, that there is now a much more frequent basic service. The trains involved were:

Time	Service	Load	Locomotive
10.35	Penzance*	12	'Castle' 5042
11.00	Wolverhampton	8/1 van	'Castle' 7037
11.35	Neyland*	10	'Castle' 5004
12.03	Paignton*	12/1 van	'Castle' 4095
12.55	Swansea	12	'Hall' 7904
13.00	Penzance	12/1 van	'County' 1006
13.25	Paignton	10	'Castle' 5087
13.40	Cheltenham*†	12	'Castle' 7000 (left 13.44)
13.47	Neyland	10	'Hall' 5932
13.58	Chester	8	'Castle' 7026
14.30	Penzance	13	'Castle' 5036
14.55	Bristol†	9	'Hall' 5979 (left 15.01)
15.05	Penzance	12	'Castle' 5015
15.13	Swansea	11	'Hall' 5925
15.25	Paignton	8	'Hall' 4941
15.40	Birkenhead	8	'Hall' 7918
15.45	Fishguard	12	'Hall' 6957
15.49	Swansea	9	'Hall' 7913
15.58	Weston	9	'Castle' 5032
16.23	Swansea	10	'County' 1007

*restaurant car provided   †combined train running in two parts

The familiar '61xx' 2-6-2Ts at work: below: No 6164 bustles along at Westbourne Park with a down semi-fast on 21 March 1959. / Michael H. C. Baker

Bottom: A smartly turned out No 6165 climbs up the flyover east of Old Oak Common across the main lines with empty stock on 19 October 1963. / Gerald T. Robinson

At a rough count, just within 6½ hours, Old Oak and Paddington had summoned up 20 locomotives (and look at all the 'Castles' earlier in the morning) and over 200 coaches. Whatever the economics of this may have been, and acknowledging that utilisation was low, the end result was remarkable. Just for the record, a parcels train also left Platform 1 during the morning, in amongst all the holiday traffic.

There were a few gems on the rolling stock side (apart from all the smart BR Mark 1 stock and GWR restaurant cars in chocolate and cream livery) such as kitchen car No 9666 in addition to another catering vehicle, but probably empty, on the 10.35 Penzance; 70ft restaurant car No 9540 (built 1907) in its customary place in the 13.15 Weston; Cunard 'Toplight' brake first No 8178 (built 1910) in the 15.05 Penzance; ex-articulated brake first No 8017 in the 15.45 Fishguard and a couple of 'Centenary' coaches. At least three GWR coaches now preserved were also in use. As usual, the WR had purloined a set of coaches from another region, but since this was not until later in the day it was excusable.

'Westerns', Stanley Raymond, Beeching and 'Hymeks' all served to change the picture during the next year, and once 1964 was out it was a different story. Change has not spoilt Paddington and the minutiae given above is recorded not for sentimentality but to give a glimpse of one enthusiast's view of the station, and to show the component parts of an overall impression of a noble station, its trains and its railwaymen.

Above: A Newbury Racecourse special of 4 March 1961 features a Cunard 'Toplight' brake first (behind the engine) and a typical GWR dining car pair in chocolate and cream livery. The train is near Westbourne Park in the care of 'Castle' No 7019 *Fowey Castle*.

Below: A typical WR semi-fast: the 19.30 Paddington-Oxford-Wolverhampton west of Subway Junction on 3 June 1959. The locomotive is No 6866 *Morfa Grange*. The fourth vehicle is one of the 1908 diners, Nos 9546-51, serving as a buffet car as far as Oxford — 103 minutes out of Paddington. / Both: Michael H. C. Baker

The Liverpool & Manchester centenary celebrations of 1930

As preparations go ahead for the celebration of the 150th anniversary of the opening of the Liverpool and Manchester Railway in May 1980, it is worth looking back to the centenary celebrations of 13-20 September 1930. These were organised by the LMSR and featured an outdoor Great Railway Fair in Wavertree Park, Liverpool, a railway exhibition in Liverpool itself and, less intentionally, a torrential downpour on the first day of the event, Saturday, 13 September. Less memorable than the 1925 Stockton and Darlington celebrations there were, nonetheless, some interesting features, principally the restoration of the L&MR locomotive *Lion*, previously rescued in 1926 from duty as a stationary pumping engine with the Mersey Docks & Harbour Board following its withdrawal from traffic in 1859. At Wavertree Park, *Lion* was used with a train of replica L&MR coaches to give rides to visitors, travelling in steam round a specially laid oval track. This replica stock was built by the LMS in 1930 and now forms part of the National Collection, being on display at the National Railway Museum, York, and

Ready to go ! Pleasantries are exchanged with the crew of *Lion* as they wait to depart on the oval passenger-carrying track at Wavertree. / *Fox Photos*

elsewhere. A complete replica 'stage-prop' train was also constructed consisting of a mock-up of the locomotive *Northumbrian* (the first locomotive on the L&MR) and the somewhat unique vehicles which formed the notabilities train on the opening day of the L&MR — 15 September 1830. This train accompanied a pageant which portrayed the history of transport up to the opening of the L&MR.

Locomotives included in the Wavertree Park exhibition were: a replica of *Rocket*; the Great Western Railway's replica of *North Star*; *Columbine*, a 2-2-2 of 1845, the first locomotive to be built at Crewe; the LNW's *Cornwall* of 1847, a 2-2-2 and Midland Single No 118 of 1899. All the foregoing have been preserved and are now treasured historic relics, many of them being scheduled to make an appearance in the 1980 celebrations. The modern locomotives shown at Wavertree Park comprised 1929-built LMS 0-8-0 No 9599; LMS Beyer-Garratt 2-6-6-2 No 4972 (both representative of recent LMS freight locomotive types and each in its own way an unsuccessful design); LMS 'Royal Scot' No 6161 *The King's Own*; the LNER's experimental four cylinder compound high pressure water-tubed boiler No 10000 of 1929 (less reverently known as the 'Galloping Sausage'); GWR 'King' No 6029 *King Stephen* (later to be renamed *King Edward VIII*) and the SR's *Lord Nelson* No E861. The last-named fraudulently appeared as E850 *Lord Nelson*; during the period of the exhibition the real E850 carried the name *Lord Anson* — E861's name. In addition, four

locomotives built by British industry for export were displayed at Wavertree and included Bagnall's No 2416, a metre-gauge 4-6-0 built for the Assam Railways and Trading Co. Passenger and freight stock was also on show.
Left: Three locomotives now happily part of the National Collection — the Midland Single, *Cornwall*, and *Columbine*, preceded by the *North Star* replica. / *LPC*

Below left: Before the celebrations opened, the replica *Rocket*, the replica *North Star* and *Columbine* receive final attention for display. / *Fox Photos*

Below: Wavertree Park on 13 September 1930. The press agency caption read, all too feelingly, 'The empty seats in the foreground give some idea of the washed out opening performance.' On display is *Northumbrian*, a petrol-propelled mock-up hauling the replica of part of the original L&MR opening ceremony's train; the leading unique vehicle carrying (as it had done in 1830) a brass band, and, next, the eight-wheeled state coach with its moulded columns and elaborately decorated and gilded finish and hangings. This had conveyed the Duke of Wellington on the opening day. Sadly, from this coach William Huskisson, MP, had fallen to his death at Parkside on the opening day. The third vehicle in this 1930 train is a replica of one of the two toast-rack carriages which had been provided for distinguished guests at the L&MR opening day. / *The Topical Press*

Below: The imperious and finely finished 'Royal Scot' No 6161 precedes LNER No 10000, GWR 'King' No 6029 and the SR 'Lord Nelson'. / *Both: LPC*

Above: LMS 0-8-0 No 9599 leads LMS Beyer-Garratt 2-6-6-2 No 4972.

The splendour of preserved steam

Above: The 'Border Venturer' of 13 May 1978 headed by '9F' 2-10-0 No 92220 *Evening Star* crosses Dent Head viaduct. / *W. A. Sharman*

Below: Midland Compound No 1000 and 'Jubilee' No 5690 *Leander* stand at York with 'The Mancunian' special for Manchester on 28 October 1978. / *J. H. Cooper-Smith*

Britannnia herself leaves Bewdley with the Severn Valley's GWR preserved stock en route for Foley Park on 10 September 1978. / W. A. Sharman

The passenger coaches of CIE

MICHAEL H. C. BAKER

If for no other reason than its colour there is no mistaking an Irish carriage. Until the early 1960s practically everything on wheels owned by Coras Iompair Eireann (CIE) was painted green. From the early 1960s this gave way to orange, with black and some white for relief. Within the same decade in Northern Ireland the Ulster Transport Authority green was replaced by Northern Ireland Railways' red, white and blue.

From dull conformity had come diversity as both railway systems experienced a colourful transition period between old and new livery schemes.

CIE carriages were also, at one time, very ancient. Indeed, just after the end of World War II, in 1948, their average age was a staggering 47, and although 10 years later this figure had been considerably reduced there were still a number of venerable antiques, including six-wheelers. But it is quite different now and no carriage in ordinary passenger service goes back before 1951, a record which I doubt can be matched by any other major European system.

Modern CIE stock is of two basic varieties, the AC stock — 73 vehicles of modified British Rail Mk 2D design numbered in the 5xxx series and put into service in 1973 — and the rest. The rest comprise a mixture of both British and Irish design and construction, numbered as follows:

Firsts 11xx
Standards (formerly second class) 12xx-15xx
Standard brakes 18xx-19xx
Catering vehicles 24xx
Bogie vans 25xx
Four-wheel vans 27xx
Post Office vans 29xx
Heating vans 31xx
Push-pull vehicles 61xx, 62xx, 63xx

The basic scheme dates back to the amalgamation of 1925 when the Great Southern Railways, CIE's predecessor, was created.

The newest vehicles, prior to the AC stock, were the two batches of heating and brake vans, numbered upwards from 3157. When main line diesel locomotives were introduced in the mid-1950s CIE, unlike British Rail, decided that train heating would be provided by special vehicles rather than from the locomotives. As a result, 52 four-wheel vans were built, 30ft long and equipped with oil-fired vertical boilers. At the same time, CIE built 63 brake vans of similar size and external appearance and the two types could be found on practically all passenger trains, particularly as CIE appeared to view passenger brake carriages as something to be avoided, only 10 such vehicles, apart from railcars, having been built between 1945 and 1970. The four-wheelers were fat, ugly boxes, looked out of place in a modern express, were unpopular with operating staff — guards would never ride in them if they could be avoided — and they began to be replaced by bogie vehicles in 1969. These were hardly less curious, being not very long (44ft 2in), slab-sided affairs of mixed European and American parentage, numbered 3157-66 and built by private contractors at the former GNR (I) works at Dundalk. They were followed in 1972 by Nos 3171-92, interesting vehicles which started out life in the 1950s as open brake thirds and brake composites on British Railways. BREL Derby Litchurch Lane works converted them to generator steam vans (GSVs), fitting them with 2,000lb/hr Spanner boilers and diesel generator sets, the latter providing the electrical power for running the boiler. They retained their original guards and luggage compartments, even down to the BR upholstery for the guard's seat. Nos 3171-92 are to be found on most long-distance trains not worked by AC stock and provide power and heating for the whole train, the carriage numbers of which bear the suffix TL (through lighting). All other carriages may be considered secondary stock although this category no longer officially exists. At one time such vehicles bore an S suffix, and later they were numbered in the 4xxx series.

The most modern carriages prior to the Supertrains — the title bestowed on the AC stock by the publicity department — were the 55 Cravens, the last of which entered service in 1968. They are the Irish equivalent of the earlier BR Mk 2s and are not unlike them in appearance and design, although going into traffic a short while before them. Their seats, of traditional CIE tubular steel framed type, are a bit primitive. In other

Above: The curious combination not so unusual in Ireland during the late 1950s and early 1960s: a modern diesel locomotive (in this case British-built) hauling non-bogie coaches. A football special composed of 16 six-wheelers, one bogie coach and a van arrives at Limerick in July 1961. / M. J. Adams

Below: An interesting line-up of CIE rolling stock in the early 1970s. (left to right) an ambulance car; a radio saloon; a 1931 GSR dining car (either No 2400 or 01) and an ex-BR standard coach, now power/heating car No 3184. / Michael H. C. Baker

Below right: A CIE express leaves Dublin Heuston. The first vehicle is a former BR coach, now a heating/brake van, then follow two Inchicore-built standards of the late 1950s, three Cravens-built coaches, two Park Royals and an Inchicore-built brake standard. / Michael H. C. Baker

respects though they are attractive vehicles, with B4 bogies, double glazing and open layout. The earlier ones were assembled by Cravens, in England, the later ones at Inchicore. All are classified as standards although at one time a few were upgraded to firsts — or superstandard as it is now known — some by the highly economical expedient of merely applying a figure '1' to the doors.

First class carriages were long a rarity on CIE and for a while it seemed as though the breed was going to be allowed to die out, none having been built since 1935. Then two, Nos 1145/6, were put into service in 1963. The last timber framed carriages to enter service with CIE they are also, to date, the last carriages built from scratch at Inchicore, and are very fine, handsomely appointed vehicles.

The non-corridor carriage is nowadays no more popular in Ireland than it is elsewhere; the last were built in 1928 and all have been withdrawn. When new vehicles were required for the Dublin surburban services in the mid-1950s, 40 carriages (Nos 1379-1418) were built, externally identical to main line stock and with corridor connections, but with vestibules instead of lavatories. These vestibules are much appreciated by passengers on the Dun Laoghaire boat trains — one of the duties for these carriages — and can accommodate a considerable amount of luggage, provided no one wants to get out before the luggage! Incidentally, the boat train was the last duty of a rake of postwar Great Northern Railway (Ireland) carriages which were taken out of service in 1971. Nos 1379-1418, and a further 10, Nos 1419-28 for main line use, are amongst the most distinctive of CIE carriages, although I would hesitate to say they were the most handsome. Designed by Park Royal Vehicles, they have straight sided vestibules with the saloon built right out to the limits of the loading gauge, very thin alloy sides with the waist rail bulging outwards, and are able to accommodate five rows of seats. They were the first Irish carriages which really looked wider than English ones. They are fitted with Commonwealth bogies, and despite 20 years' hard service they still require little maintenance, and so not surprisingly are very popular with the carriage and wagon department at Inchicore.

In recent times the oldest carriages in service were a handful of arc-roofed former Great Southern and Western Railway specimens built during the first years of the century. The last corridor example was broken up at Mullingar in the summer of 1970, but non-corridor examples were still at work in Dublin the following year. I travelled in No 4001 (formerly 845) when it was employed on the 17.52 Dublin Connolly to Bray commuter train and, although it was in a good state of repair and rode well enough, there was no doubting its 63 years. The only lighting was some incomplete gas lamps, the door catches could only be engaged by turning massive outside door handles, the seat padding — what there was of it — felt as if it might well have been original, and there was a plethora of matchboard panelling and beading around the windows. No 4001, a $24\frac{1}{2}$ton, 45ft long, eight-compartment, 96-seat vehicle was withdrawn at the end of 1971.

An infinitely loftier carriage belonging to the same era is the state coach, No 351. Originally a clerestory roofed vehicle, built in 1902 and used by the Lord Lieutenant, it later received an elliptical roof and in early GSR days conveyed dignitaries of the Church. For some years it was neglected but in 1966 it was taken into Inchicore, fitted with Commonwealth bogies, completely and most sumptuously renovated internally, given a new coat of orange, black and white paint, and put at the disposal of President De Valera. No 351 continued to serve until early 1977 when it was replaced by an AC diner, No 5406. The latter vehicle acquired some of No 351's internal fittings and was used by President Hillery when he visited County Clare in the March of that year.

In the main, Inchicore reserved the clerestory roof

for special vehicles, dining cars and the Rosslare boat train, and the arc roof remained standard until 1915. The elliptical roofed carriages built between 1915 and 1931 were generally similar in appearance, although of varying lengths, and the later ones had simplified beadings and mouldings. All were characterised by almost straight sides and rather high, fabric covered roofs. The non-corridor carriages were used extensively on Dublin and Cork suburban trains into the 1970s, but not many of the corridors were active outside the summer holiday peaks in their later years, spending a lot of their time loafing around the sidings at Connolly and elsewhere. The arrival of the AC stock finished these off, the last being withdrawn from ordinary service early in 1973.

The 32 carriages built from 1935-7 were quite different in appearance to any previous Great Southern stock, being very like the LMS vehicles of the period, even to the livery. Some were open saloons for suburban traffic — originally without corridor connections, although these were later fitted — while the rest went into service on the principal expresses, notably the Cork Mails. These carriages, too, have now all gone, except for conversions and four preserved by the Railway Preservation Society of Ireland.

The production of carriages did not resume at Inchicore until 1950, but from then until 1968 close on 300 went into service, excluding railcars and vans of various types. In essentials they resembled the 1935-7 vehicles with high, fairly flat roofs, were of both side corridor and open layout and most were either built entirely at Inchicore, or completed there from parts supplied by Park Royal or Cravens. Commonwealth bogies were first fitted around 1954, and the BR-design B4 type with the advent of the Cravens. The shape of the Inchicore-built stock changed somewhat in the mid-1950s, the flat sides from roof to waist-rail

giving way to a profile which sloped out slightly to the waist-rail, and then curved back to the underframe fairly steeply. There were, however, exceptions to this: the two firsts of 1963, for example, closely followed the earlier pattern.

A total of 200 standards was built up to 1968. Some have been withdrawn, some have become ambulance cars, some radio saloons (for use with the Radio Train), some full brakes and some standard brakes.

There were 56 composites built 1950-61. None survives in its original form, all, by 1977, being either withdrawn or converted to full brakes, first brakes, standard brakes, or standards.

Between 1953-6 Inchicore built a series of 18 buffet cars, Nos 2405-22. These are similar to the ordinary main line carriages of the period, are 61ft 6in long and 9ft 6in wide and weigh 30 tons. The counter with bar — cooking is by gas — is in the centre of the coach and flanking this are tables and individual seats for 36 passengers. All remain in service despite their displacement from principal workings by the AC stock. Prior to the arrival of the latter there were nine other carriages entirely given over to providing food and drink and six conversions from Park Royal standards. The latter had their toilets removed and replaced by pantries, which does not sound especially appealing but worked well enough, providing facilities where previously there had been nothing, eg the Dublin-Rosslare service.

The nine catering carriages proper were a mixed bunch. Two were very up-to-date: No 2402, a $32\frac{3}{4}$-ton dining car built in 1961, and No 2403, a $35\frac{1}{2}$-ton kitchen car built in 1964 and used chiefly on the Radio Train. Then there were three buffet cars inherited from the GNR(I) in 1958. The GNR had a knack of building carriages which were easy on the eye. Unfortunately, the financial and political straits which beset the company in its last years resulted in skimpy construction and poor maintenance, and although the three cars all dated from 1950, by the late 1960s they were very much the worse for wear. I remember coming across one of them, No 97N, at Inchicore in September 1969 and being somewhat taken aback to find that my fingers had inadvertently poked through its composite panelling. It survived that visit, and my vandalism, but only until the summer of 1971. The others quickly followed, No 268N achieving the remarkable distinction of never having strayed off the Dublin-Belfast main line in its entire career.

The vehicles which initiated the 24xx series, Nos 2400/1, were 64ft long wooden bodied dining cars built by the Great Southern in 1931 and rebuilt in 1935 to match the steel panelled stock introduced in that year. Other alterations were carried out over the years; they were not very handsome carriages but they were useful and were at work for over 40 years, being withdrawn the summer that the AC stock appeared. Even longer lived were Nos 2092/3. Built during World War I they, too, were modernised internally and fitted with B4 bogies, but externally their ornate panelling survived intact into the 1970s, a flamboyant reminder of a long vanished era. Both were kept hard at work until the end, No 2092 on the Dublin-Waterford line, No 2093 on the Cork Mails. When replaced by the AC stock they had spent no less than 58 years in the service of the GSWR, the GSR and

CIE. There was talk of preserving one but CIE needed the B4 bogies and the expense of replacing these with the original type would have been prohibitive.

However, it was about this time that strenuous efforts were being made in the field of carriage preservation. When I detailed preserved carriages in my *Irish Railways since 1916* (Ian Allan 1972), not one standard gauge bogie vehicle qualified for inclusion. Four years later, *Five Foot Three*, the magazine of the Railway Preservation Society of Ireland, was able to list no less than 17. This was an extraordinary achievement, brought about at the eleventh hour, since the early 1970s saw the removal from traffic of a great number of historic vehicles; but for the initiative of the RPSI nothing would now be left. My favourite, and the second to be preserved, is No 861. This is a GSWR 66ft long clerestory brake composite 12-wheeler, built in 1906 for the opening of the Cork-Rosslare route and the connecting GWR Fishguard mail boats. The epitome of Edwardiana, I knew No 861 well when as No 484a she formed half of the train which ambled between Inchicore Works and Heuston station twice a day conveying railwaymen to and from work. My only previous experience of the triple tap upon the rail joints made by her six-wheel bogies was in a sister vehicle which I came across at Waterford in the late 1950s. The very first carriage taken into the care of the RPSI was the GNR Directors Saloon, No 50, which arrived at the society's headquarters at Whitehead on the Belfast — Larne line, in April 1972. The society has five other former CIE carriages: No 1142, a corridor first built by the GSWR in 1921; Nos 1327/8, corridor thirds built by the GSR in 1935; No 1333, an open suburban third built by the GSR in 1937, and No 1335, a GSR 'wide-bellied' corridor third also built in 1937. The rest come from the GNR (I) and the NCC.

A type of vehicle which certainly deserves to be preserved is the railcar, for it served Ireland well, and continues to do so north of the Border, although no

Coaches withdrawn by CIE in the early 1970s included above far left: two former GSWR suburban non-corridors seen near Drogheda and above left: a corridor third of the 1335-38 series built in 1937. / *Both: Michael H. C. Baker*

Below: One of the 1953-6 Inchicore-built buffet cars, No 2407, in the pre-1963 green CIE livery. *G. M. Kichenside*
Below right: The impressive brake end of GSWR clerestory No 861, since preserved by the RPSI.
/ *Michael H. C. Baker*

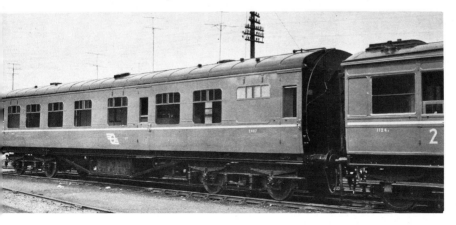

CIE example remains active in powered form. The last ones were to be seen in retirement in the shed at Bray in the summer of 1976, but some years before this the great majority had been converted to push-pull sets and as such continue to work the Dublin suburban services, powered by 201 class locomotives. Their relatively poor access does not make them ideal, and the oldest of them is past its quarter century, but they will no doubt soldier on until the long awaited electrification finally comes to ease the lot of the Dublin commuter.

The CIE railcars were slightly modified versions of the GNR (I) ones, built like them by Park Royal and with AEC engines. The GNR (I) had been pioneers of diesel railcars in the 1930s, both on the 5ft 3in gauge lines and on the narrow gauge County Donegal lines, of which they were joint owners, and a number of narrow gauge cars have been preserved at the Transport Museum in Belfast and elsewhere. Later GNR (I) cars had BUT power units and bodies built at the GNR(I) works at Dundalk, and four of these were overhauled at Inchicore as late as 1974. Someone must have changed his mind at the last minute for they never re-entered service. They have been shunted around various parts of Inchicore since then and when I last saw them in the summer of 1976 they were in same siding as a number of shunting locomotives which were being broken up, so their prospects did not seem very bright. Further vehicles of this type which had passed to NIR were regular visitors at Connolly station on summer Saturdays until replaced by new diesel-electric units in 1974.

The ambulance car is a speciality of CIE and owes its existence to the Knock pilgrimage traffic. Knock is a shrine in the west of Ireland visited by tens of thousands of Irish pilgrims every year. Many special trains are put on for them and the ambulance cars, which are carriages with stretchers, beds and other equipment for disabled people and their attendants, are a feature of these trains. The oldest ambulance car is AM12 which started out as a composite in the last year of the GSWR and was converted to its present form in 1959. In outline it closely resembles the RPSI's preserved No 1142.

The only other wooden framed and panelled carriages extant are in departmental service and these include all sorts of gems. Inevitably, Inchicore favours its own and a good many are of GSWR or GSR origin, but there are examples from the Midland Great Western Railway (second in size to the GSWR), the Dublin and South Eastern, the Waterford, Limerick and Western, and the GNR(I). There is also the former Sligo, Leitrim and Northern Counties railcar, CIE No 2509, which I saw in semi-derelict condition at Limerick Junction in 1975 and which still lingered there in 1978. Three of the best known examples of departmental stock are at North Wall: the last surviving DSER bogie suburban carriage with its distinctive parabolic shaped roof, and two former MGW corridors, one with later flush panelling, the other, a one-time ambulance coach, still with some of its engraved glass toplights. The Midland built some handsome bogie carriages, the last of them coming out under the GSR, but in many ways it was best known for its six-wheelers, which were extraordinarily long-lived, the last of them not disappearing from passenger service until the early 1960s. Some of these remain in departmental service and the RPSI hopes to preserve at least one, as well as a Waterford, Limerick and Western six-wheel saloon built in 1891.

For some time, CIE has let it be known that it requires new carriages. Negotiations were going on in the last few years with a European rolling stock builder with the intention that the carriage works at Inchicore would build carriages, not only for CIE, but also for export. Unfortunately, it now seems unlikely that this will happen. The modified BR Mk 2Ds (AC stock) have been very successful, although the Inchicore-designed interiors of the standard class leave something to be desired. Certainly, if the funds were available (which at the moment they aren't) CIE would have no hesitation in ordering once again from British Rail Engineering Ltd. If CIE is allowed the investment then the intriguing combination of British-built carriages and American built locomotives, already common on CIE, will become virtually universal.

Below: A BREL standard AC type coach makes a piquant contrast with an ex-DSER six-wheel brake now in departmental stock. / *Michael H. C. Baker*

Signalbox survey

CHRIS LEIGH

There were lots of good things about childhood train-spotting trips to Weybridge. On a summer Saturday there was an endless procession of Bulleid Pacifics pounding through the centre roads and under the high red brick arch where the Brooklands Road crosses the station. There was the almost regular sight of 'King Arthur' No 30798 *Sir Hectimere* weaving at break-neck speed round the sharp kink where the down slow line dodged the bridge pier, heading a local to Basingstoke. The gangway connections of the 'Pompey' electrics took on a fascinating swaying motion as the leading car reached the junction points, and there are poignant but less pleasurable memories of that rotten egg smell sometimes emitted by the Bulleids, and the all-enveloping sandy dust of the local footpaths. As locals, we knew all the best vantage points, and a particular favourite was on the road down to the Heath Bridge. Here the road was level with the signalbox upper floor, and as the box had windows in the rear wall it was possible to listen for

Above: The 'bobby's' viewpoint. The signalman at Uffton Crossing box, near Aldermaston, replaces the distant to caution behind the 10.30 Paddington-Plymouth on 6 March 1970. / *D. E. Canning*

the bell codes and then watch the approaching train as the red lights flicked along the illuminated track diagram in the box.

Sadly, the Weybridge signalbox has now gone, and one must admit that from an architectural viewpoint it was not really very startling. It was a typical half-timber, half-brick structure in SR green and cream, with a predominance of that rather over-yellow cream of which the Southern was fond. However, I was much impressed by SR signalboxes and the distinctive examples which survived from the London and South Western Railway were particular favourites. These were generally substantial brick-built structures with distinctively shaped window frames, and often the main front windows were bisected by a solid brick panel, inside which the instruments were mounted.

21

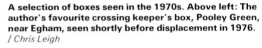

A selection of boxes seen in the 1970s. Above left: The author's favourite crossing keeper's box, Pooley Green, near Egham, seen shortly before displacement in 1976. / Chris Leigh

Above: A GWR standard box at Lavington, near Westbury, has come to the end of its working life in October 1978. / D. E. Canning

Left: Marsh Brook box on the Shrewsbury-Hereford line is likely to survive for a little while and looked in good shape in October 1977. / John Scrace

Below: The typical Midland Railway box at Uffington, between Peterborough and Stamford, makes an interesting contrast with two Class 20s on a freight during 1978. / Laurie Manns

Below right: Early in 1973 the Preston power signalbox spelt the end for the LNW Preston No 4 box, an excellent example of a standard design being stretched almost infinitely. / British Rail

Large window areas were essential to most manual signalboxes, and consequently the designers often made window frames a distinctive design feature. The Great Western, for instance, made widespread use of sliding frames containing five panes (three small, above two large), while the LSWR had curved tops to the upper panes and the Midland had angled corners. Early boxes on the GWR often had oval 'toplights' above the main windows, while the Lancashire and Yorkshire used rectangular toplights and carried the main window area down almost to floor level.

Despite closures and widespread resignalling it is still possible to find LSWR signalboxes in use. The fine example which stood in the centre of Virginia Water station has now gone, along with my favourite crossing keepers' box, at Pooley Green, near Egham. Luckily, I acquired the track diagram and capstan wheel for posterity. Incidentally, even without the weight of the gates and linkage this wheel is no lightweight to turn, and it is small wonder that signalmen were not too keen on the frequency of trains and road traffic in the rush-hour! Another nice example of this type of box, again complete with gate-wheel, was situated on the end of the single platform at Barnstaple Town, but as long ago as 1972 this was deserted and vandalised.

The influence of LSWR design evidently spread to its little neighbour, the Midland and South Western Junction Railway, with its cross-country line from Cheltenham to Andover. At the north end of Swindon Town station was a little box of similar design, curiously built against the cutting wall. This was a marvellous station in perfect harmony with its red brick surroundings, and had once had a licensed refreshment room. At Wolfhall South Junction the M&SWJR opened another LSWR-type box on 6 September 1905, but the company's home-spun design was usually executed in timber and distinguished by fancy barge boards and finials. The one at Cricklade had a brick base, a few steps, a porch, and a balcony extension at one end, and was most attractive. The M&SW called its boxes 'cabins' and Cirencester retained this title to the end, even when fitted with a GW-type cast nameplate. The only survivor, to my knowledge, is at Savernake High Level, where the box stands disused in the grounds of a bungalow formed by adapting the station building.

The Midland Railway also built its own standard pattern timber signalboxes, and survivors can still be seen although, as with most types, resignalling progress is gradually wiping them out. The characteristic features of these boxes were a hipped slate roof, narrow vertical boarding above the windows, and a precarious looking wooden walkway around the front of the box at first floor level. One such box was sited at Longbridge, a station which lost its through services as long ago as 1928 but which remained open until the 1950s for workmens' trains to the Austin Motor Company, This box was, and probably still is, the hub of the British Leyland works railway system. A branch from the Midland line near Northfield serves the plant and handles supplies of steel and sand for the forges, fuel oil for machinery and outgoing shipments of cars and metal waste. It was a late stronghold of steam where one could find the two big Bagnall 0-6-0STs (now at the West Somerset Railway) and a Kitson 0-6-0ST (now at Llangollen) working alongside Class 25 diesels.

At its northern end the Longbridge line joined the Great Western at Halesowen, and here, although the

station was closed, the signalbox and goods yard remained in use during the 1960s. The line to Longbridge had by then been severed to enable the demolition of Dowery Dell viaduct. Halesowen signalbox was built on the station platform, was small and well kept and retained its tall, floor-mounted single line staff machine at this time.

The sturdy red brick signalboxes which were the standard GWR pattern from the turn of the century will be familar to most readers. There were some examples built entirely in wood, and luckily a few still exist, although by chance the preserved ex-GWR lines seem to have inherited a rather unbalanced mixture of styles. Here, the standard brick boxes with their classic five-paned windows (three small panes above two larger ones) are almost in the minority, with Buckfastleigh on the Dart Valley, and Blue Anchor on the West Somerset as probably the only ones on working lines. That at Bridgnorth is a rebuilt structure with an untypical join between the old and new sections, but another example, at Llangollen, is being restored. The West Somerset also has a timber standard box, which originally came to the line from Maerdy and for many years served at Dunster level crossing. Latterly it has been moved to Minehead. Among the other preserved examples are pretty but non standard types at Bewdley and Highley on the Severn Valley, and an original Bristol and Exeter Railway box at Williton on the WSR.

Heading west from the Midlands one came upon a strong London and North Western influence on the former Shrewsbury & Hereford lines (GW & LNW Joint) and then pure LNWR on the Central Wales line. There was little evidence of the Great Western among the original architecture on the S&H although footbridges and standard fittings appeared later. In these situations curiosities often arose and the architectural 'offspring' of such mixed marriages were often remarkably attractive. Tenbury Wells, for instance, appears as a solidly LNWR version of a Great Western country station, but the best feature was the distinctly un-Great Western combined waiting shelter and signalbox. The box had to be tall to provide a view over the roof of the shelter, and the unusual red tiled roof was almost pointed.

Many other curiosities existed up and down the country and there is space to mention only a few. At Lydford, where the GWR and LSWR lines ran side by side, the two signalboxes were incorporated in a single structure. This rarity was pure London and South Western from one side, and typically GW from the other! The box at Dawlish has a narrow base with a curved overhang at the front. Because of its famed seafront position legend suggests that the design was intended to throw back the waves before the windows got broken! A more likely reason is the simple need to save space on the already narrow platform. At Dolgellau the GWR had an end-on junction with the

24

Left: The station at Wolferton, used by the Royal Family when visiting Sandringham, was one of the most elegant and best kept in the British Isles, but was closed with the demise of the Kings Lynn–Hunstanton branch. Architecturally, it was untypical of the Great Eastern Railway, as exemplified by the unusual and highly decorated signalbox. / *Dr R. Preston Hendry*

Two signalboxes from a more recent era. Above: The SR 1930s style box at Twickenham. / *John Scrace*

Above right: The utilitarian wartime GWR structure of Oxford North Junction box (now replaced). / *Gerald T. Robinson*

Cambrian Railways and the shared station had one platform in GW style and the other in classic Cambrian complete with the 'fish-shaped' canopy decorations. Similarly, the boxes at either end of the station were in their owner's distinctive styles.

Bucknall, on the Central Wales line, was an LNWR delight, with its cottage style station building bedecked with Tudor porches. The extremely wide level crossing gates were controlled by a little LNWR box that was one of the nicest on the line. At the opposite end of the LNWR scale, the illustration of Preston No 4 shows how a standard design can be stretched to exceptional proportions.

Although the largest boxes could be impressive through sheer size and the smaller ones were often quite pretty, the signalbox was essentially a functional building. The architecture was seldom elaborate, and decoration was normally limited to wooden finials and fancy barge boards. Inside, the flooring was generally stained boards or perhaps a plain terra-cotta linoleum with a few sticks of utilitarian furniture. The signalmen could make their surroundings quite palatial by providing personal touches, and of course the gleaming polished instruments and levers reflected the attention to detail and routine which was the essence of the job.

At Wolferton, where the Great Eastern Railway built its station to serve the Sandringham estate, an elaborately decorated signalbox was provided. In addition to the barge boards and finials, decorative trim boards were provided at the front and back, and the end gables were hung with interlocking coloured tiles. A couple of nice patterned rugs are also evident in the illustration.

While it may not be too difficult to decide which mechanical boxes were the largest (Newton Abbot East with 206 levers is the largest in current use), the smallest boxes are not so readily identifiable. Among today's power signalboxes, of course, there are many which in terms of movements and area controlled are larger than Newton Abbot East, but the miniaturisation of equipment and switches has enabled the latest boxes to be built to quite modest proportions. Indeed, sophisticated electronics enable one signalbox to cover many miles of line, with only an array of lights to show the location of trains, so that windows are now largely superfluous.

The smallest boxes and ground frame huts are really nothing more than a simple shed, and one of the neatest that I recall was the ex-Cambrian Railways box at St Harmons on the Moat Lane–Brecon line. It was a tiny wooden structure with a small window in the front, and scarcely room to turn round inside it. The little Lynton & Barnstaple Railway's narrow gauge line through a delightful part of North Devon had a basic signalling system and small signalboxes were provided at Lynton, Barnstaple, Chelfham and Bratton Fleming. The box from the latter station was moved some time after the line closed and to this day forms an ideal timber garden shed. Tucked away in the woods, it retains its faded green paint and the remnants of an SR notice.

All the signalbox designs mentioned so far have had their origins in the pre-Grouping era, but new signalboxes were built by the 'Big Four' and some of these, too, were of distinctive design. From the early 1930s the Southern Railway was at great pains to project a 'modern' image to accompany its widespread electrification programme and with the rebuildings the latest materials and techniques were used. Foremost of these was reinforced concrete, and the SR even

devised a type of concrete paling fence to replace timber at many stations. The SR signalboxes built to match this modernity were masterpieces of contemporary design which have stood the test of time. They were built in a combination of red brick and concrete with the upper storey having rounded ends. Among the many examples of this design, some of which still exist, were Horsham, Arundel, Bognor Regis, Woking and Twickenham.

The Great Western boxes of this period were as bad as the Southern ones were good. Initially the GWR experimented with the use of alternative materials for construction of the standard box. The five-paned windows and general style remained the same, but composition blocks and asbestos panels were tried. Examples of the last appeared at Marlborough on the ex-MSWJR line, and at Taplow, the latter having been demolished only a couple of years ago. The resulting boxes looked rather cheap and nasty, but the GWR — in the interests of economy — then went worse still and produced the ultimate in austere signalboxes. Several appeared at wartime yards, notably around Oxford, and some still exist. The walls were of pink Fletton bricks and were devoid of any detail or decoration. The window frames were metal and a flat reinforced concrete roof was the finishing touch. After nationalisation the Western Region produced a number of neat plain timber boxes in red cedar and there were examples at Hungerford, West Drayton and Shiplake.

The LMS produced a substantial new signalbox at Manchester Central in 1935 to replace a dilapidated timber structure. The new box was built on a frame of steel girders to raise the operating floor above surrounding obstructions, and the structure itself was a bay-fronted brick affair. Most new boxes on the LMS were built after nationalisation in connection with WCML electrification, although there was also a standard manual box design which was very neat. Prewar and early postwar LNER designs tended to be a rather squarer version of the SR style, but the best looking modern boxes in the east were those built during the fifties. These imaginative structures at places such as Pelaw, Potters Bar and Hadley Wood consisted of a brick-built locking room, often in blue or grey brick, with a glassy operating room in which the big windows were raked outwards at the top. Some of these signalboxes were displaced all too quickly by resignalling schemes.

Although a wide variety of signalboxes survive on preserved lines, and many mechanical boxes in use on BR will last into the next century, the signalbox is at a definite disadvantage where building conservation is concerned. Stations can often undergo tasteful conversions to other uses, while small goods sheds (surely the most neglected of all railway buildings from the conservation viewpoint) can sometimes find new usage as warehouses or light industrial premises. Even so, there are some fascinating survivors such as on LT's High Barnet branch where the ex-GNR signalboxes are in use as railway stores. Signalboxes, however, are usually too close to running lines or too inaccessible to be sold for other uses, and indeed their inherent shape and size limitations make conversion difficult. Add to this the fact that removal of the ground frame usually necessitates demolition (the author once watched contractors remove the frame from Launceston SR box through the roof, without taking off the roofing first!) and it is easy to see why the traditional signalbox has disappeared so quickly. The examples which remain will become as treasured a part of the railway preservation scene as the steam locomotives they served.

Narrow gauge

sand in Norfolk

R. A. KING

At the end of July 1977 one of the last narrow gauge industrial railways in East Anglia ceased to function. The line at the British Industrial Sand quarry at Legiate was east of where the old M&GN line from South Lynn to Melton Constable crossed the GER line from Kings Lynn to Swaffham. Both these lines are closed to passenger traffic, but sand trains still regularly travel the 3½ miles from BIS's private siding at Middleton Towers to Kings Lynn.

At one time there were up to 15 locomotives on the 2ft gauge system which connected the quarry with Gaton Road (M&GN) and Middleton Towers (GER) stations. But over the last few years the system has gradually been replaced by conveyors for collecting the sand and taking it to the plant near Middleton station. The railway was left with the job of taking the stones and other waste from the plant for dumping, but this too was taken away in 1977.

On hearing that the system was closing down I re-visited it and was shown round by Mr Lionel Ragg, the works manager. I was just in time to photograph the remainder of the system before it was cut up.

The track to the two-road locomotive shed had been removed, but behind the warehouse I found a row of locomotives Nos 23/5/6 (works nos MR11298, 60s317/8) with No 24 (MR11297) nearby on the main

Above: Better days for British Industrial Sand's 2ft gauge railway at Legiate, Norfolk, in June 1974. Locomotive No 25 heads a rake of skip wagons from the quarry towards the plant. / R. A. King

line. Weighing about seven tons these four-wheeled diesel-mechanicals were all built by Motor Rail, Simplex Works, Bedford, between 1965/6.

Much of the track in the plant was still in place, together with the main line leading under a minor road and into the quarry. Mr Softly, the railway foreman, told me that all the track was due to be removed in a few weeks, a railway society having some but the rest was to be scrapped.

The rolling stock on the line was mainly four-wheeled side-emptying skip wagons with a few flats used for track maintenance. All the 50 or so skips were stored in a row near the plant awaiting their fate.

But one bright spot was that No 22, a Simplex of 1954 vintage (MR No 11003), was expected to be used for some time on an isolated length of track in the quarry to haul six skips of stones a few hundred yards for dumping. But on the day of my visit I found the locomotive had over-run the end of the track and was buried axle-deep in sand.

27

Left: When the railway was still operating, No 26 passes under a minor road and into the plant. The main line was double track, narrowing to a single line to pass under the road. A conveyor can be seen on the left.

These next two scenes are dated 1 August 1977. Below: A row of skip wagons at the rear of the BIS plant. In the background, the replacement conveyors rise triumphant. Bottom: Meanwhile, behind a warehouse lie out of use locomotives Nos 26/25 and 23. / All: R. A. King

Inter-City, or not?

All pervasive though British Rail's Inter-City brand name may be, it is sometimes difficult to define the extent of its applicability. Sir Peter Parker has talked of BR's 'crumbling edge of quality' and certainly there are examples where services have been downgraded in the last decade or so; conversely, others have made upwards progress, but still compare unfavourably with the Inter-City service standards of the TV commercial or publicity leaflet. On this page both the services depicted are uncertain in status. Above: The 07.15 Nottingham-Glasgow headed by 40.120 past Dent on 20 September 1978 represents a truncated Midland route service over the Settle & Carlisle line. / D. E. Canning

This picture: The Paddington-Worcester through service was at one time threatened altogether; at other times dmus were suggested. Over a stretch of line with two-way working, 47.121 arrives at Worcester (Shrub Hill) with the 18.45 Hereford-Paddington on 20 May 1978. / Les Bertram

One up, two down. Above: The 10.15 Birmingham (New St)-Norwich on 1 July 1978 in the hands of 25.047 and leaving Thetford is an example of a route upgraded from one-time all dmu services. / John C. Baker

Below: Oban-Glasgow through services have been threatened more than once and have now been stripped of any prestige. 27.037 arrives at Taynuilt on 22 March 1978 with the 12.55 Glasgow (Queen St)-Oban. / John Sagar

Right: In 1970 the North and West route was downgraded and its cross-country expresses diverted. Near Marsh Brook, south of Church Stretton, a Class 25 proceeds with the 13.45 Crewe-Cardiff in July 1977. / A. Eaton

Above: The 18.55 (Sundays) Manchester (Piccadilly)
-St Pancras train threading the Hope Valley near Hope
behind 45.147 in June 1978 was a last and undistinguished
survivor of the Midland Railway's service between
Metropolis and one-time Cottonopolis. / L. A. Nixon

Below: The Bristol-Portsmouth service plumbed the depths
in the mid-1970s but has since been revived a little, as
exemplified by the 13.20 Bristol-Portsmouth in the charge
of 33.030 at Southampton on 25 October 1877. / G. R. Jelly

North London services over the GNR

ERIC NEVE

An interesting chapter in London suburban railway history was closed when passenger trains between Broad Street and Great Northern line stations were withdrawn on 7 November 1976, following the introduction of electric services from Moorgate (LT) to Hertford North and Welwyn Garden City.

Over the first quarter century of GNR operations in the London area great changes occurred in traffic patterns, posing severe strains upon the very limited facilities originally provided in the Kings Cross vicinity. Looking back it would seem that the promoters of the Great Northern Railway did not realise just how local traffic would develop following the opening of the main line to Peterborough and beyond in 1850. This lack of foresight, together with the acute financial stringencies imposed at the time, resulted in insufficient tracks and allied facilities being installed in the early years. Until 1861 the first station out of the GN's London terminus was Hornsey, four miles away. In 1861 two wooden platforms were erected at Seven Sisters Road — $2\frac{1}{4}$ miles out — to serve seven trains each way on Mondays to Fridays, plus one extra down train on Saturdays and about three Sunday trains. Such was the modest beginning of Finsbury Park, destined to become the GN's busiest station in later years with 10 platform faces, eight running lines, six signalboxes and numerous carriage sidings. The name Finsbury Park was adopted on 1 January 1870.

October 1863 saw the start of GN suburban trains serving Farringdon Street, reached by means of the Metropolitan Railway's Widened Lines. These trains were extended to Moorgate in June 1869. Additional suburban traffic had been generated by the opening of the Edgware, Highgate and London Railway in August 1867 which was worked by the GNR from the outset. This line joined the GN at Finsbury Park and was the trunk to the Northern Heights branches of later years. By 1873, the GN was working local trains over the branches to Edgware, High Barnet, Alexandra Palace and Enfield. In the wake of extensive house building, passenger traffic increased enormously and, coincidentally, there was a progressive build-up of coal, merchandise, cattle, fish and meat traffic from the northern parts of the expanding GN system and beyond.

Inadequate facilities at the London end caused acute delays, particularly at the approaches to Kings Cross where only one up and one down running lines existed. Delays were frequently caused by goods trains destined for Kings Cross goods yard having to cross both running lines on the flat at Maiden Lane (later to become known as Belle Isle). In 1862 connection had been made from the goods yard to the high level North London Railway line at Maiden Lane. By this means traffic for the GN's City depot at Royal Mint Street (close by the Fenchurch Street terminus of the London & Blackwall Railway) was taken by the NLR via Canonbury, Dalston and Bow. As a means of alleviating this congestion the GNR Board had authorised construction of an additional Copenhagen tunnel to the west of the original bore and reached by means of a flyover at Holloway — as a result all trains for the goods yard would be kept clear of the main running lines. Both flyover and tunnel have been adapted to carry outer suburban electric trains to and from Kings Cross local station to avoid conflicting movements which would delay Inter-City trains using the terminus. In the event, completion of the new Copenhagen Tunnel was delayed by financial restrictions until 1877. Meanwhile, in 1872, an Act was obtained for a line (1 mile 32 chains in length) from Finsbury Park to join the existing NLR at Canonbury Junction which would enable goods traffic to travel direct to the London Docks and Royal Mint St. Relief was therefore afforded at Kings Cross with the opening of the new line in 1874. But delays to suburban trains continued to annoy season ticket holders so much so that a protest meeting was called by a well-known resident of Seven Sisters Road, Samuel Waddy QC, MP. At the meeting in the City Terminus Hotel a resolution was passed for a deputation to wait upon the Directors of the GNR to discuss improvements in the service.

Now the 1872 Act for the Canonbury line had also empowered the GN to gain access to the Broad Street terminus of the NLR, therby making it possible to provide a service of GN passenger trains into the heart of the City, as well as affording relief to the existing Widened Lines Moorgate services. However, there was an important proviso: not only must the GN obtain permission from the NLR to operate such a

service, but it also needed the blessing of the powerful London & North Western Railway. The last-named had both a large financial stake in the NLR and a lease on part of the Broad St terminus. From the very beginning of the GNR, the LNWR had pursued an implacable policy of non-cooperation with the East Coast company, so, not surprisingly, Euston flatly refused to give assent to running powers for the GN to use Broad St. But with pressure from season ticket holders boiling up, the GNR board was obliged to seek the best bargain possible. In time, a compromise emerged with an agreement by which NLR trains would operate from Broad St to certain destinations within the GN suburban area. Payment was to be made by the GN on the basis of a fixed sum per train

mile to cover haulage, and the provision of rolling stock and train staffs, together with customary mileage proportion of all through fares as well as rent for part of the Broad St terminus. As a partial offset for this hard bargain, the GN would also begin exercising its running powers for goods trains between Canonbury Junction, London Docks, Poplar and Royal Mint St.

All arrangements were concluded in time for the new passenger service to start on 18 January 1875 when a total of 12 weekday trains were run, six each to High Barnet and New Barnet. From 1 February of the same year, adjustments were made to the GN's Moorgate service and no less than 34 NL trains then operated — 16 to High Barnet and nine each to

Above left: The GNR's station at High Barnet, down the hill from the town centre, is the location of this view of a standard North London Railway 4-4-0T, No 47, built at Bow in 1865 and seen after its second rebuilding.
Left: Into Hadley Wood, north of New Barnet station, comes a down NL train for Potters Bar headed by a standard NLR 4-4-0T. / Both: Rixon Bucknall Collection/Ian Allan Library
Above: The NLR tanks had to contend with some fierce gradients on the GNR's Finsbury Park–Highgate section to the tune of 1 in 60, here obviously causing NLR 4-4-0T No 1 to raise the echoes near Crouch End with a train for Muswell Hill. / Rixon Bucknall Collection/Ian Allan Library

Enfield and New Barnet. A further increase in operations came with the opening of the Alexandra Palace line in May 1875 when seven trains commenced running to that ill-fated terminus. A Sunday service of 10 trains commenced in June. From Broad St the mileages over the GN were: High Barnet, 13.25; Alexandra Palace, 8.75; Enfield, 10.1, and New Barnet 11.0 miles.

The furthest point on GN metals reached by NL trains was Hatfield (19.75 miles from Broad St), the town being served in August 1877 by one return train leaving Broad St at 18.48, stopping at all the 11 intermediate stations then existing and taking 61mins overall. Return from Hatfield was at 20.27. This train lasted only until November 1878, but in May/June 1879 another train worked to Hatfield, leaving London at 13.55. July 1883 saw another short-lived Hatfield train as a result of the 10.32 Broad St-New Barnet being extended. Noteworthy in having only 5min turn-round time at Hatfield, the train was curtailed at New Barnet after only four months. Some 43 years would elapse before Hatfield was again served by trains from Broad St.

Potters Bar was first used as a terminus for NL trains in July 1880 by extending the Sunday 16.25 ex-Broad St on from New Barnet and by the end of 1881 there were two regular workings to Potters Bar. Thereafter this station was served continuously until

NL trains ceased operating over the GN in 1940.

A feature of the service in the mid-1880s was the omission of intermediate stops by selected peak hour trains. The 16.39 Broad St-High Barnet, for instance, was non-stop to Finsbury Park, and then called only at Finchley to reach High Barnet in 34min. The 08.48 from Enfield omitted all stops to Wood Green and was non-stop thereafter to Finsbury Park before calling at Canonbury, Milday Park and Dalston Junction to reach Broad St at 09.17. The last stage involved a smart 5min sprint from Dalston despite the 1 in 60 climb up to Haggerston and the 15mile/h service slack at Shoreditch.

In September 1888 no less than 62 trains were booked on weekdays from Broad St to GN destinations between 06.05 and 22.55, serving Finsbury Park (6 trains), Alexandra Palace (5), East Finchley (2), Wood Green (1), High Barnet (18), New Barnet (7), Potters Bar (4), and Enfield (19). One afternoon train on Saturdays terminated at Bowes Park. On Sundays a total of 13 return trains ran and, with due respect to the 'Church interval', none started between 09.25 and 13.18. Six went to High Barnet, three to New Barnet and four to Enfield. The maximum number of NL trains over the GN reached 65 in 1906 and was still 63 in 1910, by which time rapid growth of London's electric tramways had begun to erode traffic.

To facilitate operation over the heavily used section of line from Dalston into the city terminus, many of the trains from GN stations were booked non-stop between Finsbury Park and Dalston Junction, then fast into Broad St; 11min only were usually allowed for the distance of 4.4 miles. One notable train in 1910 was the 08.39 ex-East Finchley which ran non-stop from Stroud Green (08.48) to Shoreditch (08.59) reaching Broad St at 09.02. Some idea of the intensity of the morning peak service may be gauged by the fact

Above: Devons Road, Bow shed's LMS '3F' 0-6-0T No 7490 takes a six coach set of LMS 57ft non-corridor stock — built for Broad St-GN services in 1930 — up to Potters Bar on the double track bottleneck of the GN main line. These coaches provided first, second and third class accommodation until 1938. / *Ian Allan Library*

Left: Close-up of an ex-North London four-wheeler seen here in LMS livery in the early 1930s. LMS No 6439 is a five-compartment second and is working in a Poplar-Broad St set. / *Alan Whitehead*

Right: Some time between 1938-40, LMS '3' 2-6-2T No 105 works hard beyond Potters Bar Tunnel with a train bound for Potters Bar formed of a 1930-built LMS set. / *Eric Treacy*

that 21 GN line trains were booked into Broad St between 08.15 and 10.02, all having to share the two tracks into the station from Dalston with other NL services from Chalk Farm and beyond and Bow and Poplar trains. For homegoing City workers, the 19.11 from Broad St called at Dalston Junction, Mildmay Park and Canonbury to reach Finsbury Park in 13min. Running fast to East Finchley from Finsbury Park, it reached High Barnet at 19.49. Today, of course, the High Barnet line commuter has an unvariable diet of Northern Line tube trains from Moorgate via Camden Town.

Successive curtailments occurred during World War I which heralded the decline of the GN/NL services. The Sunday service, for instance, was

withdrawn from January 1917, never to return. After the Armistice there was a gradual revival in frequencies but never again would the total of trains reach the peak achieved in 1906. After Grouping, matters continued more or less as before under the aegis of the LNER and LMSR and the year 1929 may be taken as the peak for postwar operations. Then, the weekdays only service totalled 44 trains (with five extras on Saturdays) running to Alexandra Palace (10 trains), High Barnet (13), New Barnet (5), Potters Bar (3) and Gordon Hill (13). The Saturday extras went to High Barnet (3), Potters Bar (1) and Hatfield (1). Gordon Hill, a once-familiar GN suburban train destination, had become a terminal point from 4 April 1910 when the Enfield branch was extended to

Cuffley; from then until 1918 only one lone North London train travelled to Cuffley.

Some interesting points of the 1929 service involve empty coach workings. In the morning six empty trains ran either from Broad St or Canonbury to various GN stations to form up trains, two being notable in that they went to East Finchley only to form the 08.39 up (still running as in 1910) and the 09.07 which called at all stations to Finsbury Park, and then only at Dalston to reach Broad St at 09.32. At this time two up morning trains omitted Finsbury Park altogether — the 08.39 from Finchley Church End and the 09.00 ex-Alexandra Palace. Unusually, the two East Finchley trains mentioned above had started from Highgate in previous years. Another empty train ran from Canonbury at 07.23 to Cuffley to form the 08.21 to Broad St. Curiously, in the evenings there were only two empty workings and both were from Alexandra Palace; one of these conveyed passengers to Finsbury Park only, and was then run empty to Broad St.

Notable down evening peak trains included the 17.07 to Potters Bar, allowed just 2min to take water at Finsbury Park and then promoted to run on the fast line non-stop to New Barnet, afterwards passing through the Hadley Wood bottleneck ahead of the 17.30 Kings Cross-Newcastle express. The 17.07's timing was understandably amended in 1935 to start at 17.15 so as to reach New Barnet (on the slow line)

just after the prestige streamlined 'Silver Jubilee' had passed. In practice, this timing put some strain on the locomotive so the start was altered to 17.12 and 3min were now allowed at Finsbury Park for water. Arrival at New Barnet was at 17.40 so allowing $2\frac{1}{2}$min for a 'blow-up' before following the 'Jubilee' through the Hadley Wood bottleneck.

Detailed changes only occurred over the next decade so that by 1939 there were three fewer trains run in the week but one more on Saturdays. Each weekday in the last days of peacetime the first morning departure from Broad Street was at 06.05 and the last at 20.12, both to High Barnet. The first up train left Gordon Hill at 07.05, being formed from an empty stock working. Indeed, these first and last times had endured for very many years with little alteration.

With the outbreak of war in 1939 the entire LMS service to and from GN stations was suspended on 11 September. A restricted service was resumed on the following 4 December when there were but 14 departures from Broad St SX, and 10 SO. Only three trains started from Broad St in the mornings, while three more started at Finsbury Park and there were two empty stock workings to outer points forming City-bound trains for the morning peaks. The evening service commenced at 15.22 and ended at 18.20, while on Saturdays seven trains started from Broad St between 11.55 and 13.57. In all, Monday-Friday departures were to High Barnet (5 trains), Alexandra

Above: After July 1945, the Broad St-GN line trains were usually formed of GN and LNER quad-art sets worked by 'N2' 0-6-2Ts, although 'L1' 2-6-4Ts and 'B1' 4-6-0s also appeared at Broad St. A typical evening commuter service from Broad St-Hertford makes its approach to Finsbury Park behind 'N2/2' 0-6-2T No 69528 on 13 May 1954. / Brian Morrison

Below right: In the last year of Broad St-GN line services, a Cravens-built dmu forming the 09.11 Gordon Hill-Broad St is glimpsed near Canonbury on 13 May 1976, having come on to the North London proper at Canonbury Junction. / Kevin Lane

Palace (4), Gordon Hill (6), Potters Bar (2), and, on Saturdays, High Barnet (3), Alexandra Palace (3), Gordon Hill (6), and Potters Bar (1).

Following severe damage by enemy action to most parts of London's East End, the GN services from Broad St. were suspended from 4 October 1940, although the LNER timetable dated 28 October indicated a ghost service on only a slightly reduced scale from the previous one. But not until 30 July 1945 did passenger trains from GN line stations once more serve Broad St and from then until 1976 all were operated by the LNER and its successors, so that the link with the NLR was no longer apparent.

The NLR services had indeed remained distinctive between 1875 and 1945, by virtue of the locomotive and rolling stock. Until 1923 the NLR trains were hauled exclusively by 4-4-0Ts of some six main varieties dating from 1855 up until 1907. In 1923 the LMS inherited 74 of the original standard NLR 4-4-0Ts with outside cylinders, all built at Bow Works between 1868-96, and to these it allotted LMS Nos 2800-73. In addition, there were four surviving inside cylinder 4-4-0Ts of 1860s' Adams design, of which LMS No 2874 was still at work on the NL trains over the GN lines until its demise in 1925. The other three tanks of this type had earlier been acquired by the LNWR and given the numbers 2647-9. These three were at Willesden shed and so did not usually find employment on GN line trains, but No 2647 was seen passing Hadley Wood on a Potters Bar train on Saturday 12 May 1923. The NLR 4-4-0Ts had not long to live and all inside cylinder examples had been withdrawn by early 1925 with the outside cylinder version disappearing by 1929. Few of the latter ran with LMS numbers but two (Nos 6444/62) did, with the added glory of red livery.

During 1923/4 the LMS conducted extensive trials with ex-LNWR 0-6-2T ('Coal Tank') No 1009 on NL passenger duties over the GN, but the ultimate choice fell on the standard LMS '3F' 0-6-0T, more usually

regarded as a shunting engine. About 1933, however, some trials were made with Fowler 2-6-2T No 15550 which was seen on both Gordon Hill and Potters Bar trains. The 0-6-0Ts, popularly known as 'Jinties', soldiered on unaided until March 1938 when Devons Road shed (Bow) was allotted four Stanier 2-6-2Ts Nos 79/82/105/55 for use on the Broad St to GN line trains. Following some trials on a Sunday (when LMS trains did not usually operate over GN lines) the Stanier tanks took up regular duties alongside the 'Jinties'. The first recorded working was on 21 March 1938 when No 155 headed the 17.32 Broad St-New Barnet and thereafter both 0-6-0Ts and 2-6-2Ts covered the workings until services ceased in 1940.

In the 10 years after the 1923 Grouping the rolling stock for GN services mainly comprised 13-coach rakes of North London origin dating from 1884. These four-wheeled, flat-roofed, close-coupled sets were made up of a full brake, six thirds, three firsts, two seconds and a full brake — reading from the northern end as leaving Broad St. Although electric lighting was provided, the third class seats had no upholstery to the backs, which were only shoulder high between compartments. There were 15 such sets still in use in early 1933, numbered between N1 and N21. Three other set trains were held in reserve, being used infrequently. These three, numbered N2, N5 and N13, were of LNWR origin having been built at Wolverton for the Richmond service from which they were displaced by electrification in 1916. The vehicles were also four-wheelers but had normal partitions in the thirds. The set formations were: brake third, five thirds, four firsts, two seconds and a brake third. The high proportion of first-class accommodation may well have been the reason for infrequent use of these three trains. Of these sets, No N5 was unique in retaining its NLR teak livery and NLR numbering.

From mid-1933 the LMS commenced withdrawing this ancient stock in favour of more modern bogie vehicles. There were seven sets of LMS-built coaches made up into rakes of six (brake third, two thirds, third/first composite, first/second composite and brake second). Half of this allocation was made up of wood panelled stock and half was steel panelled, and eventually they received the set numbers N7/10-12/6-8. Additionally, there were seven sets of ex-Midland Railway stock in seven-coach rakes (brake third, two thirds, one first, one first/second composite, and a brake second). These MR sets carried the numbers N1/3/4/6/8/9/15. At the time, and until abolition of second class accommodation in 1938, these 14 set trains must have been the only ones providing second class on the LMS system.

Regular travellers from GN line stations to and from Broad Street — once described as 'the daylight route' to the City since the number of tunnels was small in comparison with the GN's Widened Lines Moorgate line, or the Great Northern & City tube from Finsbury Park — will always remember the spartan conditions endured for so long. Enthusiasts, viewing matters in a different light, were often entertained by races between LNER and LMSR trains when leaving Finsbury Park for the north. In particular, one remembers the 18.05 Broad St-New Barnet leaving Finsbury Park at 18.22 alongside the 18.15 Kings Cross-Cambridge and Peterborough. The former was non-stop to New Southgate and usually had the better of the Gresley 'K3' 2-6-0 on the Cambridge/Peterborough train until Hornsey was reached, after which the 'Jinty' gradually fell behind.

In the main, there were few out-of-course events during the 65 years of North London workings into GN territory. The most notable, without doubt, was the collison on 10 December 1881 in Canonbury Tunnel resulting from a signalman's error which involved four trains. A less publicised event occurred on 20 June 1924 when the 4-4-0T hauling the 08.44 High Barnet to Broad St suffered a 'blow-back' approaching Totteridge station forcing the crew to take refuge outside the cab while the engine ran out of control. The driver fell off near Woodside Park but the fireman gallantly managed to re-enter the cab and to bring the train to a halt before it reached Finchley (Church End). His action prevented an otherwise inevitable collision with a preceding train.

Today, however, electric traction, of uniform formation, rules supreme on the former GNR lines once served by North London trains. The High Barnet branch, part characterised by London Transport modernisation of the 1935-40 programme, and part reminiscent of its GNR origin, sees only aluminium-clad tube trains while the Alexandra Park branch has long since lost any services. Meanwhile, on the Hertford loop and on the GN main line itself, services are provided by the Class 313 inner suburban units working to Moorgate via the Great Northern & City 'tube'. Broad Street, once the scene of so much activity, slumbers on, awaiting incorporation into a new Liverpool Street.

When a thousand flowers bloomed

ROGER FORD

Left: Two main line diesel locomotives forming part of British Rail's Modernisation Plan stand side by side at Saltley Depot in November 1977. (left) a Class 47 of Brush/Sulzer parentage, the logical successor to the earlier Class 46 (right) also with similar genesis and power equipment, but with BR workshops' mechanical parts. / Noel A. Mackell

Hindsight, according to Sir Peter Parker, is the most beautiful sight in the world. True enough, there are always occasions when we wish we knew then what we know now and British Rail's motive power policy since nationalisation is a particularly fruitful field for this type of exercise. However, for such hindsight to be salutary one has to obey certain rules. There is little point in condemning an unfortunate engineer for his choice of motive power just because we know that after 10 years' hard work the bogies start to crack because of faulty welding when they were built. But there is value to be had from considering decisions and relating them to what ultimately befell, provided that criticism or acclaim is based only on what was known at the time. Thus, in retrospect, the change from steam to diesel traction under the 1955 Modernisation Plan is seen to contain a good selection of inferior designs which have gone to the scrapyard well before their allotted span. The good locomotives are with us still, though growing long in the tooth. It is clear to us now which were sheep and which were goats — but could it have been foreseen then? The answer, as this article hopes to show, has to be 'yes'.

Today, it is easy to forget that the Modernisation Plan was not solely concerned with motive power. Indeed, the total value of the Plan was £1,240 million of which diesel locomotives for main line use represented £125 million. And it must be remembered that in those days you could buy a 2,000hp locomotive for under £100,000 compared with around £600,000 for a Class 56 freight locomotive today. With such large sums of money involved, and limited experience of main line diesel traction at home, BR made the reasonable decision to try out various designs of diesel locomotives in revenue-earning service before buying in bulk. And this is where the trouble started. BR launched their technical revolution with the same attitude as Chairman Mao's cultural revolution in China several years later. Mao proclaimed 'Let a thousand flowers bloom' and found that he could not cope with this sudden relaxation of state control. BR, with a handful of British firms building diesel locomotives, ordered 14 different types for evaluation under the pilot scheme with almost every combination of engine and transmission.

But before the proliferation of designs is examined, there is the matter of the horsepower ratings. Under the pilot scheme, diesel locomotives were divided into three classes. Class A was 800hp-1,000hp and was intended for freight; Class B was for general purpose duties and covered 1,000hp-1,250hp; while, for the heaviest main line passenger and freight workings, Class C provided 2,000hp-2,300hp. The pilot orders covered 28 Class C units, 90 Class B and 60 Class A locomotives of 1,000hp or less. Hindsight immediately queries the preponderance of low-powered units.

41

Three locomotive designs of greater than 1,000hp exported by British industry prior to the evolution of the Modernisation Plan diesels. Above: One of the first big diesel locomotives to be ordered by overseas customers, a 1,600hp 1A-Do-A1 for Egyptian State Railways, is seen here under construction at English Electric's Preston Works. / GEC

Below left: Only six years after the Egyptian locomotives went into service, English Electric had applied 2,000hp to a 3ft 6in gauge locomotive — for Rhodesia. Two of these 'DE2' Class machines take a Botswana and Mafeking freight out of Bulawayo in the late 1970s. /Rhodesia Railways

Below right: Twenty-five 1,254hp A1A-A1A locomotives were supplied to Ceylon from 1952-5. The mechanical parts were built at Bagnall's works at Stafford and completed at Brush, Loughborough. / Brush

Right: What might have proved a significant early star did not turn out that way. This was 827hp Bo-Bo No 10800 with North British mechanical parts, Paxman engine and BT-H electrical equipment. In this view it takes a demonstration train through Kilburn on 14 November 1950.
/ E. R. Wethersett/Ian Allan Library

Partly, the rating of the general purpose machines reflects the lighter, slower trains of two decades ago and the multitude of freight trip workings then existing. But more significant is the fact that locomotives with a fairly precise power output were being ordered to replace steam locomotives which had no such thing as a nominal horsepower rating. By mortgaging the boiler and giving the fireman a 'wet back' a steam locomotive could be given what a diesel engineer would call a 'sprint rating'. The diesel, however, was limited to its installed power. Thus at a comfortable steaming rate of 15,000lb/h a 'B1' or a BR Class '5' gave a drawbar horsepower of about 800 at 30mile/h falling to 600dbhp at 70mile/h. However, at the maximum steaming rate of 20,000lb/h this rose to 1,100dbhp at 30mile/h and 1,000dbhp at 70mile/h. In an attempt to reconcile this fundamental difference in rating, locomotives were compared in terms of tractive effort. Thus a 1,000hp Class 20 diesel with a maximum tractive effort of 42,000lb and a continuous rating of 19,500lb, or a Class 27 with ratings of 40,000lb maximum and 25,000lb continuous, seemed a fair replacement for a general purpose steam locomotive such as a 'Black 5' with a quoted tractive effort of 25,455lb.

The confusion over ratings illustrates a very important point of the Modernisation Plan as far as motive power was concerned. The customer who was buying the locomotives had less experience of diesel traction than some of his suppliers. While steam remained king on Britain's rails, a number of UK manufacturers had been exporting electric and then diesel locomotives for a generation or so. In the course of this work, a considerable fund of experience had been acquired on matching the new motive power to the duties involved and not by comparison with the steam locomotives it was replacing. Thus, while in the pilot scheme locomotives of around 1,000hp predominated, for overseas railways higher horsepower diesels were being built in British factories. In 1948

English Electric had delivered 1,600hp 123-ton locomotives to Egyptian State Railways. These had been followed by 1,760hp 121-ton diesels for South Australian Government Railways in 1950, 1,500hp 90-ton units for Queensland Government Railways in 1953 and more 1,500hp locomotives for New Zealand in the same year. At the time that the pilot locomotives were ordered, English Electric was building a 2,000hp narrow gauge diesel-electric weighing 113 tons. Other well-known names were also exporting diesels. Brush Bagnall had started supplying 1,254hp 87-ton units to Ceylon and Birmingham Railway Carriage & Wagon was building locomotives powered by the six-cylinder Sulzer engine at ratings around 1,000hp for Ireland and Australia.

So, in addition to the six prototypes on British Rail (Nos 10000/1, 10201-3 and 10800), there was a fair amount of home-grown experience available and, through its licence, Vickers could also draw on Sulzer's diesel traction experience. Here was the nucleus of a diesel fleet which, while not technically exciting, would provide reliable motive power for years. Hindsight bears out this judgement; today, all British Rail diesel locomotives from the 350hp Class 08 shunter to the latest Class 56 3,250hp freight locomotive are powered by Sulzer or English Electric engines. Yet to get from logical start to logical finish was a very convoluted business at a not inconsiderable cost in money, manpower and operating problems.

Instead of concentrating on proving under BR conditions those types successfully being supplied overseas by UK firms, the British Transport Commission went for safety in numbers and gave almost every potential manufacturer a chance to learn at its expense, irrespective of prior experience. Perhaps the most unusual aspect of the pilot orders was the advent of the diesel-hydraulics. Remembering that screams of pain had arisen at the suggestion that BR should buy General Motors locomotives from the USA, or build them under licence, it was indeed odd

that three of the types ordered should have had German engines and transmissions. True, these would eventually be built under licence (with the inevitable problems as the licensee learned the hard way of the various 'tricks of the trade' which did not show up on the manufacturer's drawings) but it was a different technology derived for a different type of railway.

Going through the list of engines specified brings up the problem of instructive and destructive hindsight. There is no doubt that the Sulzer 6LDA 28 was a safe bet. The engine was running in Ireland and British manufacturers were already using it. The 12LDA 28 lacked home market experience but 35 units were running at 2,000hp on French Railways and its satisfactory performance could be deduced from the good behaviour of its six-cylinder brother. The 12-cylinder Sulzer also offered 300hp more than the English Electric 16-cylinder unit which by then had developed more muscle from 1,600hp in Nos 10000/1

to 2,000hp. As with Sulzer, the English Electric engines were traction proven in various cylinder configurations. Incidentally, the two English Electric locomotive designs in the pilot scheme (nowadays Class 40 and Class 20) had the added advantage of being built entirely by the same firm — mechanical parts, diesel engine and electric transmission. Significantly, these were the only pilot scheme locomotives that were the product of a single manufacturer.

But the other diesel engines, we now know, were not suitable for BR's operating conditions. However, this was not apparent at the time, even to the most sceptical observer. Perhaps the biggest surprise was the decision to re-engine all the Mirrlees-powered Brush Class 31s with English Electric engines at a cost of around £4 million. This type of Mirrlees engine ran, indeed continues to run, satisfactorily overseas and only started to crack after several years' of BR service.

The photographs on these two pages record some of the less happy aspects of early Modernisation Plan diesels. Above: When seen here at Cambridge in 1964, these two Brush Type '2' (now Class 31) still retained their Mirrlees engines. / G. R. Mortimer

Left: The Metrovick Co-Bos were ill starred. In their early days they worked Anglo-Scottish freight and then filled in on Scottish passenger trains such as this Glasgow-bound express leaving Stirling on 8 August 1959. / M. R. Galley

The Crossley engine fitted in the Metropolitan Vickers asymmetric Co-Bo (and also used in Ireland) was a low speed engine at 650rev/min when everyone else was running at 850-900rev/min. It also took eight cylinders to do about the same work as the Sulzer six. The remaining two home-built engines were both long shots. The Paxman engine in the BTH/Clayton and North British 800hp locomotives was a 16-cylinder unit running at 1,250rev/min. By any standards it should have been a non-starter in the rail traction business where a basic adage is to get the power you need from as few cylinders as possible. Nor was its 'sewing-machine' nature suited to the rudimentary maintenance which the first diesels would receive from a railway struggling out of the steam age. Finally, there were the 10 'Baby Deltics'. Today, the Class 55 'Deltics' can be seen as the one stroke of brilliance in an otherwise mundane diesel programme. But while they shine in hindsight, at the time they were highly controversial. While the 18-cylinder 'Deltic' engines could be tolerated because they made possible the most powerful diesel locomotive in the world, there was no way in which a more highly rated nine-cylinder version of the engine could be justified in a small general purpose locomotive.

As for the electrical equipment in the locomotives, there was much less room for debate. Some manufacturers had more experience than others, but the big rationalisation of the electrical industry was looming on the horizon and by the time some of the pilot series locomotives entered service BTH for one was no longer a proud, independent name but part of one of the growing empires. For the mechanical parts' builders it was also a time of change. With steam locomotive manufacture, the builder was largely master of his fate. Nearly 50% of the steam locomotive by value represented material and 32% labour. With the diesel locomotive, material costs

Above: The 'Baby Deltics' did not approach the prowess of their bigger brothers. D5901 leaves Kings Cross with a Cambridge line semi-fast. / Eric Treacy

Right: The North British/Paxman/GEC combination produced the 800hp D84xx class which was short lived. / R. J. Buckley

English Electric had put itself in a strong position by 1955 with the acquisition of Robert Stephenson & Hawthorns Ltd and Vulcan Foundry. RSH's Darlington works turned out some export locomotives in the late 1950s such as this 1,000hp diesel–electric for Argentine State Railways, powered by the 8SVT engine. / *GEC*

represented 70% and labour only 10%. This reflected the large amount of equipment which a firm who produced only mechanical parts had to buy in. Nor was it simply a case of buying in engines and transmissions. New skills had to be learned — control engineering, coolant systems and what today would be called systems engineering — the bringing together of the various sub-systems in a working whole.

Once again, English Electric had taken a lead by acquiring such famous locomotive building firms as Vulcan Foundry and Robert Stephenson & Hawthorns and converting them to diesel and electric traction manufacture. Significantly, the assimilation took place in the year of the Modernisation Plan. Brush was taking the first steps to self-sufficiency and BRCW was building locomotives for export. Faced with the inevitable change in the scheme of things, one of the proudest names, North British, had been building up a diesel lcomotive capability since 1948. The first stage was a licence for the German Voith hydraulic drive and, in the year before the pilot scheme

orders were placed, this was followed by a licence for the German MAN engine. The power of NBL at the time can be judged from the fact that it supplied four designs for the pilot scheme — more than any other firm. It was clearly a management to be reckoned with and there was a strong case for the diesel-hydraulic locomotives it could build. In place of the lumbering giants such as BR's homegrown 138-ton Class 44, German Railways were running the first V200 2,000hp diesel-hydraulics weighing only 80 tons in 1955. Clearly, the established British diesel locomotive manufacturers were out-of-step and out-of-date. When the British Transport Commission specification resulted in the NBL 2,000hp diesel-hydraulic weighing 117 tons a further design was added to the pilot scheme menagerie — a Swindon-built version of the V200 with yet another engine design (the V12 Maybach) and Mekydro transmission.

Even at the time, there were rumblings about the sheer number of designs to be evaluated and the lack of traction experience of some of the engines. Even

allowing for political forces there were more firms involved than there needed to be, or achievement justified. Today, the combination of eight different engine makes, eight transmissions and eight mechanical parts' builders certainly seems more like idle curiosity than a determined drive to find a fleet of basic designs which would meet BR's needs and, equally important, work reliably under BR's operating conditions and standards of maintenance. Even without discarding those designs which hindsight tells us were losers, it is still possible to produce a shopping list which would have taught BR engineers more and at less cost.

As a Chief Mechanical Engineer determined to make the change to diesel traction effective and painless what would the writer have chosen for a pilot scheme? Because operating experience had already shown the value of the high horsepower locomotives the 2,000hp English Electric design could be justified in larger numbers from the start as the base for a large class. If the pilot scheme was to be of value there would have to be a yardstick and the Class 40 was the obvious choice. With the Rhodesian locomotives under construction putting 2,000hp into 113 tons it would be nice to think that I would have had the vision to ask for a Co-Co. As a back-up to the English Electric design, and for the higher power ratings promised by Sulzer, a similar number of 'Peaks' would have been ordered from BR workshops — say 20 of each class. In the 'B' range the Sulzer 6LDA 28 engine

Above: North British had experience of diesel locomotives for home and overseas. This sort of press photo was beloved of the manufacturers. A 625hp diesel electric with GEC electrical equipment is bound for Ceylon Government Railways in 1951. Below: But for NBL to act as the main contractor was a different matter. This is the prototype 2,000hp diesel-hydraulic for BR's Western Region under test, in incomplete livery, on the Glasgow-Kilmarnock line on 27 November 1957. / G. A. Dick

was the prime candidate and, as BRCW had experience of the engine, this company was the natural choice to be what the Navy calls the 'lead yard'. Once again, a back-up would be wise, not only as an insurance against trouble, but to ensure the supply of enough engines when building began in earnest. Brush, with its 1,250hp locomotives for Ceylon, selects itself.

This still leaves the CME with three areas to cover. One is the 800hp locomotive. Working on the fewer-cylinders-the-better principle, the obvious power unit is the English Electric six-cylinder engine. This had

As putative CME the author would have chosen.
Left: the Sulzer 12LDA 28 powered 'Peaks' for the pilot scheme. In this view, D10 *Tryfan* makes a rare appearance at Aberdeen, waiting to leave for Glasgow in August 1960. / E. W. H. Greig

Below : He would also have selected the six-cylinder Sulzer 6LDA28 engine and chosen Birmingham RC&W as main contractor for the 'B' category locomotives. D5314, now Class 26, typifies this combination and is seen here in May 1959 at Welwyn Garden City on the 12.25 Kings Cross-Cambridge. / N. Caplan

Right: Doubtless there would have been no alternative but to build a 2,000hp diesel-hydraulic locomotive in the 'hindsight' pilot scheme. Here, a pristine Swindon-desgined B-B, 'Warship' No D805 *Benbow*, brings the up 'Cornish Riviera Express' through Liskeard station on 23 May 1959. / M. Mensing

Bottom right: An intriguing tailpiece. Few big diesels were exported from the UK in the wake of the Modernisation Plan. Ten were 2,700hp locomotives built by English Electric for Portugal in 1968/9, the others were 'hush-hush', export versions of the Brush/Sulzer Class 47s which were built by Clayton Equipment, delivered to Cuba in the mid-1960s. With train identification '0Z00' No 2503 for Cuba is seen on Midland metals on test.

originally powered the 350hp shunter on the LMS (which ultimately became the standard BR design) and now in turbocharged Mk II form would provide the 800hp specified. The second area is North British, and the company is inevitably tied up with the third area — hydraulic transmission. Here the dividing line between the prescience the author likes to think he would have shown and the benefit of hindsight becomes very blurred. Yes, NBL must have work, and the spirit of the times demands that alternatives to the established 'British' diesel-electric locomotive must be tried. The two NBL 1,000hp designs actually ordered meet both these requirements with direct comparison possible between the Voith hydraulic transmission and the electric equivalent. Of course, the big claim for hydraulic transmission, and the German diesel-hydraulic concept as a whole, was that it enabled lightweight, high-power locomotives to be built. With the forces behind the hydraulic lobby we would

probably have had to build the 'Swindon' 2,000hp B-B based on the Deutsche Bundesbahn's V200, even though its eventual adoption would mean setting up new licence building arrangements for the Maybach engine and Mekydro transmission, but not the NBL 2,000hp design as well.

So there we have a master plan for a rational pilot scheme. Had it happened that way would it have changed the course of dieselisation on BR? The answer has to be 'no'. The original plan behind the pilot scheme was that the prototype batches would be run for three years before mass orders were placed in the light of this service experience. This would have involved keeping steam traction in service until 1970, which Continental experience indicates would have been perfectly feasible, particularly if the remaining steam traction had been kept in particular regional areas and concentrated on freight duties. But had BR kept to this course of action, and not made the

gadarene rush for dieselisation en masse, it would have had little effect on subsequent events. This was because of the basic fallacy of believing that running diesel locomotives on the steam railway was a reliable indicator of long-term performance. Thus, for example, it was not until the Brush Class 31 was put on to services based on its true potential, and not those of the steam locomotives it had replaced, that the Mirrlees engines started to develop cracks. Jumping ahead in time, it was not until the HST started operating diagrams built round a 125mile/h railway that crank case cracking became a problem. All that the pilot scheme would have proved after three years was that the manufacturers concerned could build locomotives which worked quite well on light duties and when cosseted by the user and the manufacturers' site engineers.

But, the pilot scheme was not an entire waste of time. It gave a head start to some of the best of British Rail's workhorses which have provided a nucleus of reliable motive power when, at times, railway engineers must have wondered whether the Modernisation Plan was worth the trouble. The 'Peaks' and their successors still give sterling service, particularly on the orphan Midland main line where they run to surprisingly fast passenger schedules despite the handicap of supplying electric train heating. The 'Forties' whistle on forever and are now becoming a cult class. The BRCW Class 26 was the forerunner of a series of successful designs powered by the Sulzer six-cylinder engine. When re-engined the Brush Class 31 became even more useful thanks to an additional 220hp, while the lowly-powered Class 20 is an efficient and reliable mover of heavy freight trains

when worked in multiple. In this 25th anniversary year of the announcement of the pilot scheme hindsight tells us only that companies who have experience of designing, building and then operating equipment in service conditions have a better chance of producing something which works properly than newcomers to the business. The pilot programme was not the first time that this lesson was learned on the railways nor was it the last.

Reading by Southern

The existence of the Southern's Reading station next to the GWR's Reading General always made train watching interesting in this important Thames Valley town. In the mid-1960s, however, the variety was soon finished Steam haulage on the Reading-Redhill-Tonbridge service generally ended as from 3 January 1965, although isolated workings continued into that autumn. Then, as from 1 March 1965, the WR took over control of Reading Southern and from 5 September of that year new platform facilities at Reading General saw the diversion of the Redhill route and Waterloo-Reading electric trains into the WR station. Today the site of Reading Southern is a car park. Enthusiasts of an earlier generation will feel that the real interest on the SR lines to Reading ended with the electrification of the Virginia Water via Ascot to Reading route as from New Year's Day 1939. The camera of E. J. Crawley records the variety of train working before the Waterloo trains went electric.

Above: Actually a post-war scene, of 26 April 1948, this view of Reading SR shed records a particularly characteristic Reading line type, ex-SE&C 'F1' 4-4-0 No 1028. Behind is SE&C 'R1' 0-4-4T No 1696, left is SR 'U' 2-6-0 No 1628.

Bottom: A visitor from far-off Exmouth Junction shed, ex-LSW 'T9' 4-4-0 No 117 takes the 12.55 Reading-Waterloo out past Reading's gasworks on 11 April 1938.

Oppposite page, right: Unusual at Reading at the time, ex-LC&DR 'T' 0-6-0T No 1602 reposes on shed on 31 May 1937.

Centre right: Ex-SE&C 'C' 0-6-0 No 1068 at the head of a Trio 'C' set forming a Saturdays only Ash-Reading train near Earley on 4 June 1938.

Below right: Representing the third SR pre-grouping company, an ex-LBSC 'C2x' 0-6-0 leaves Reading with an up goods on 14 October 1938.

More Reading area shots from the camera of
E. J. Crawley. Above: The conductor rails are already in
position as ex-LSW 'M7' 0-4-4T propels an auto train
formed of ex-LSW 'gate' stock out of Reading on
21 October 1938.

Left: Unusual use by the GWR of its train identification
plates for this GWR '43xx' 2-6-0 No 6327 at the head of
LNER stock making up a race special returning from Ascot
on 15 June 1938.

Below: Star on the SR lines to Reading was the through
Birkenhead-Dover train and typical motive power was
SR 'U' 2-6-0 No 1639 taking the southbound service out
of Reading on 21 June 1937.

The Hope Valley Line

RAYMOND KEELEY

A breathing space between the gritstone southern
extremity of the Pennines and the northern dales of the
Derbyshire limestone country comes in the shape of
the serenely beautiful Hope Valley. Well it might be
named for the railway that weaves its thread to link
one end with the other. Decisions of closure and
change, a decade or so ago, had the effect of saving
this lovely stretch of line. But survival in this valley
was at the expense of rail travel in other valleys which,
in their own way, are equally interesting.

I have known the Hope Valley line for many years,
more especially at the time when it was considered a
poor alternative to the Woodhead route between
Manchester and Sheffield. Twenty-five years ago, the
journey could take up to $2\frac{1}{2}$ hours, whereas, even in
steam days, the journey on the Woodhead line lasted
barely one hour. Occasionally, a helpful ticket
examiner at Sheffield Midland would advise: 'Nip
smartly across to Victoria, sir — there in half the time,
this one stops at every siding!' How does one answer

*Above: Hope Valley idyll. Sunlight picks out the details of
the 06.05 Manchester (Central)-Sheffield (Midland) as it
attracts early morning custom at Bamford on
28 September 1955. Motive power is a 'Jubilee' 4-6-0.*
/ R. E. Vincent

the logic of that? Certainly I never tried to explain the
virtues of riding behind an ancient Midland 4-4-0
which was probably creaking at every seam, and
breathing steam from every pore.

Nowadays the Hope Valley line sees hourly interval
Manchester-Sheffield expresses and a stopping train
service between New Mills and Sheffield. There is a
bonus too, for the mid-afternoon is crowned by the
passage of a train which, if publicity and imagination
played its game to the full, could equal the flamboyance
and mystique captured by the 'Orient Express' in its
heyday. But, alas, the Harwich (Parkeston Quay)-
Manchester Boat Train passes in almost complete
anonymity, hauled by a Class 45 or 47.

In the days of steam the journey on this line began

53

in that huge cavern of glass and iron which constituted Manchester's Central station. An awesome place where the sound of steam and trains entered a new dimension, each footfall, every buffered clang and clatter of coupling became magically amplified. The feeling of dignity, of destiny, was overwhelming, giving a sense of momentous occasion to the beginning of any journey.

To match the majesty of this great railway station, at least 20 years ago you may have hoped that the head of your train would be graced by that noblest of locomotives, a Midland Compound. I had real affection for the Compounds which became deeper with the passing years; to me they symbolised Midland grace and elegance, even though the voice was somewhat rumbustious. The deep bass voice coming as a gruff bellow at the first clearing of the throat never failed to surprise, and so unexpected from an engine, which although relatively large and powerful, managed to suggest it would prefer you to notice elegance rather than muscle power. Fortunately there is a marvellous disc of Compound sounds which includes a few superb shrieks and whistles at Central.

A spectacular exit from Central carried the lines on a lofty brick viaduct, then high girders and these, on massive cylindrical support columns, crossed a complex of canal and industry in huge strides. Height was then gradually lost until at Cornbrook the lines drew level with the parallel Manchester-Altrincham (MSJ&A) lines, where a crossover enabled the Chester trains to join the Altrincham line. All track from Central to this point is now lifted but the structures remain, comprising viaducts, bridges and the colossal shell of the station.

Cornbrook remains a junction. Here the lines from Manchester Oxford Road (which has now replaced Central) split, the Altrincham-Chester lines veering away south-west, the Liverpool lines going west on the bed of the old main line from Central. After a few hundred yards on this route, a further split saw the old Midland/Great Central lines curve away south-east to dive under the MSJ&A and head for Chorlton. Soon after the latter, at Chorlton Junction, the Great Central line turned east, the Midland continuing in a south-easterly diagonal across the Manchester suburbs towards Cheadle Heath. The old Midland line is now lifted to a point just north of Cheadle Heath station. At Heaton Mersey (the station before Cheadle Heath) a short connecting spur allowed the Sheffield stopping trains to join the Altrincham-Stockport line of the old Cheshire Lines. From there, using the northern bank of the gradually narrowing Mersey valley, the line is soon burrowing through red sandstone outcrop at its narrowest point and then, in tunnels and cutting, passes close to the town centre to emerge at the platforms of Stockport (Tiviot Dale).

Tiviot Dale was a charming little station standing almost at the conflux of two rivers (a couple of hundred yards to the east the rivers Goyt and Etherow combine to form the Mersey) and was noted for the pride of the station staff. The sense of importance in their call — 'Stockport-Stockport!' — belied its size, especially as the much bigger and busier main line station, a half mile away, was just plain Edgeley. The lovely old station buildings at Tiviot Dale have been destroyed but the platforms still exist.

Hard work now for the Compound as it climbed steeply to gain the higher ground between the valleys. The CLC line to Woodley was left behind at Bredbury Junction, the engine continuing the upward grind to come parallel with the GC/Midland Reddish-Romiley line joined just before entering the latter station.

Romiley, an interesting station complete with most of the original buildings and a vintage Midland signal box, stands at the apex of a triple junction. This consists of the two lines just mentioned and that from Hyde Junction via Woodley. The spur from the Stockport-Woodley line, just used by the Compound, is now lifted but the others remain in use. At Romiley old and new routes merge: the present-day trains for Sheffield now start at Piccadilly, using the Ashburys-Reddish line. A convenient place, then, to change the tense of the narrative. Past and present can easily mingle especially as the topographical splendours to come are just as firmly present today as they were 20, or even 100 years ago.

Mention of the Hyde Junction route reminds me of what is probably the most exciting development of the 1970s to affect the Hope Valley Line. I refer of course to the steam hauled specials. These trains — there seem more of them as each year passes — are usually steam hauled between Guide Bridge and Sheffield, joining, via Hyde Junction, the route about to be described at Romiley. With long tunnels, scenic splendour, and a switchback route of heavy gradients, a more thrilling 30-odd miles of railway does not exist in England. The late 1970s and early 1980s will, one hopes, see the presence of some of the nation's most prestigious steam locomotives. What more superb spectacle could there be than a Bulleid or Gresley Pacific struggling manfully towards Chinley South Junction, a sight almost guaranteed to raise the beetling brows of the ever brooding Cracken Edge. I

Above right: The author's favourite Hope Valley line motive power — a Midland Compound. LMS-built No 41118, recently ex-works, gets attention from its fireman as it waits at Manchester (Central) with the 13.04 departure for Chinley.

Right: Sheffield express 1976. A dmu crosses the River Goyt at Marple. The river is below the girder section. / Both: R. Keeley

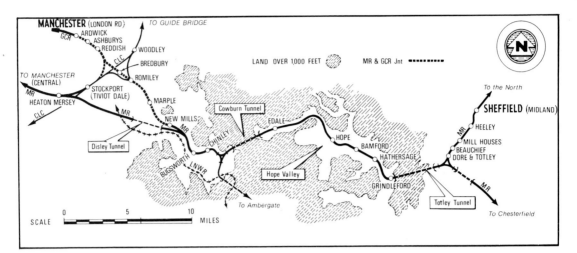

MANCHESTER (LONDON RD)   TO GUIDE BRIDGE
GCR   ARDWICK
         ASHBURYS
         REDDISH   WOODLEY
                    BREDBURY
TO MANCHESTER   ROMILEY
(CENTRAL)
MR   STOCKPORT
HEATON MERSEY (TIVIOT DALE)
                    MARPLE
CLC   MR   NEW MILLS
                         CHINLEY
         Disley Tunnel
                    BUGSWORTH LNWR
                                      Hope Valley
                                   To Ambergate

LAND OVER 1000 FEET   MR & GCR Jnt ----------

Cowburn Tunnel
              EDALE
                    HOPE
                         BAMFORD
                         HATHERSAGE
                              GRINDLEFORD

To the North

SHEFFIELD (MIDLAND)
         HEELEY
         MILL HOUSES
         BEAUCHIEF
         DORE & TOTLEY

                         Totley Tunnel
                              To Chesterfield

SCALE   0   5   10   MILES

have stood atop the latter on days long past when the tall column of smoke and steam from a 'Jubilee' could be traced almost all the way from Chinley to Doveholes Tunnel on the Millers Dale line. However, fortunately this can still be experienced with *Scots Guardsman* and several others, but towards the other tunnel at Cowburn. However, we had better return to Romiley, or I will throw the whole narrative out of sequence.

For the first mile out of Romiley the line uses low embankment or shallow cutting, then, after a short stretch of deeper cutting, the rails seem to launch into space, but in reality are supported by the solid stone of a high viaduct. This is Marple Dale, providing one of the most beautiful views that I know from a railway viaduct. South-west, a deep, lush, heavily wooded dale. A dense mass of trees covers the valley sides from top to bottom almost completely screening the River Goyt which winds its way along far below. In the foreground the Peak Forest Canal strides the dale on a massive stone aquaduct. This superb monument to the canal stonemasons' art has only recently been restored to something like its original condition, yet already the mindless hand of the graffiti artist has been at work.

The view north-east is more open giving distant vistas of windswept hilltops. It is hard to believe this picturesque spot is barely 10 miles from the centre of Manchester. But even amid the beauty there are blemishes, as in many other places in the land — modern industry and commerce have much to answer for.

Within yards of leaving the viaduct, the train crosses Marple Wharf Junction, to the left the signalbox, and on the right the line to Marple (Rose Hill), while our line continues south-easterly. Within a few seconds it will tunnel under the canal, which, although below us when crossing the dale, has not commenced its long climb through a flight of locks

Below right: During the mid-1960s steam power could be found powering holiday trains over the Hope Valley line. LMS '5' 4-6-0 No 44851 of Trafford Park shed climbs up towards Chinley North Junction on the slow lines with the 09.45 (Saturdays only) Manchester (Piccadilly)-Yarmouth (Vauxhall) on 2 July 1966. / *John Clarke*

until it sits high on the shoulder of Marple Ridge.

The exit from the tunnel brings the platforms of the one-time important station of Marple into view. Only one of the original buildings remains and this, an attractive Midland signalbox standing on the up platform, proclaims the station's GC/Midland origins. The box is sagging a little now as if to show the burden of age, a fact emphasised by the absence of other buildings and platform awnings.

Beyond the station the line follows a heavily wooded course for about one mile and then leaps a narrow gorge in a single dizzy span. Beneath flow the waters of the Goyt, with a brief glimpse to the north of the so-called Roman Lakes. Immediately below, on the south side, can be seen an intriguing octagonal shaped house and a waterfall, these, and the lakes, being evidence of the late 18th century activities of Samuel Oldknow.

Another Midland box at Strines is one of the half dozen that still exist between Romiley and Chinley. Rumour has it that an intention to replace them with a new power box at Romiley has been shelved.

The valley narrows considerably at the approach to New Mills, a small town with what appears to be a disproportionate amount of railway. The concentration of three separate railway lines with river, canal and roads, is caused by a pincer movement of hillsides which nip the valley to create an hour-glass shape.

The position of New Mills Central station is quite

striking, being balanced almost precariously at the entrance to a narrow defile, on the northern, more precipitous, encroachment of hillside. From a junction south of the platform ends, lines veer left and right into tunnels. Those to the left reach a dead end in the tunnel and what was the beginning of the Hayfield branch (closed January 1970) now used for stabling dmu turn-rounds on the Piccadilly-New Mills service.

Beyond New Mills the railway curves sharply south to meet, in about a quarter of a mile, the old direct main line from Manchester Central coming in from the east. A crossover adjacent to New Mills South Junction box gives access to the old main line. Beyond the crossover the New Mills line became the slow line as far as Chinley North Junction but this is now lifted as far as Chinley Station South Junction. The old main line now joined, the line follows the River Goyt south for a short distance before making a determined eastward turn towards the formidable hillside barrier cradling the western end of the Vale of Edale. Across the valley the LNWR Buxton branch is clearly seen on its comparatively level section between New Mills (Newtown) and Whaley Bridge. In Midland Compound days you would probably look out for the chance of seeing a Fowler 2-6-4T bowling along this stretch, on the branch they had dominated since the early 1930s and continued to do until the dmus took over. The view east shows the extensive, though now sadly desolate, site of the one-time Gowhole sidings,

on the far side of which the track-bed of the slow lines passes in a shallow arc.

The eastward turn on a great curve is into a high, wide cutting, opened out from a double-bore tunnel when the line was quadrupled in 1902. The gradient is severe, something like 1 in 90, the combination of curve and steep rise always seeming a difficult proposition for the Compounds. If they should slip — well, there would be a right old fuss; an angry, deep-throated roar from the chimney, immediately followed by a jangle from motion and coupling rods. Seen from the carriage window it was like watching the struggles of an old horse that has slipped between the shafts of its wagon: hooves clatter, the legs are splayed in a valiant attempt to get back on four feet.

Part of the station buildings and the down platform of the long-closed station at Buxworth can still be seen at the east end of this impressive cutting, then, in hardly more than a mile, comes Chinley, grand junction of the Peak.

Chinley! What a name to conjure with, but, alas, not any more, for the grandeur has gone, and so has the junction, at least in the passenger sense. What remains seems like acres of desolate platform space in a wasteland almost devoid of buildings. A sad contrast to the place my friends and I knew 20 years or so ago, when a seeming abundance of platform staff ministered to the passengers' needs. I can still hear their strong vocal exhortations — 'Chinley, Chinley,

change here for Derby, Leicester, St Pancras', or 'Chinley — next stop Manchester Central', and many variations on the theme. Chinley, like all great railway stations, exuded a civilised air, when even the start of a local journey captured a sense of occasion. The sensation of moving into the next unknown, albeit tiny, segment of life can still, however, be strongly felt on some railway platforms.

There are splendid views from the embankment following the first overbridge after the station. To the north the ever brooding Cracken Edge stares across at the distinctive 'mountain in miniature' peak of South Head. The saddle connecting the two gives shape and form to a short but lovely valley lying between them seen in grandstand view from the carriage window. The south prospect is dominated by the pyramid of Eccles Pike (a shape seen even more effectively through the rear window of the dmu in the last few hundred yards before Cowburn Tunnel) beyond the east flank of which is seen the flat edge of Coombs Moss and the sharp drop of Castle Naze.

At Chinley South Junction the old main line to Derby swings away south to face a great barrier of hillside penetrated by the dreaded Doveholes Tunnel. The Hope Valley line turns north-east to face the same formidable land mass. This is really an immense saddle linking Kinder Scout — the huge peat bog fist of gritstone upland and a final segment of Pennine backbone — with the limestone uplands of Derbyshire. It is also a great divider of waters, for the streams and rivers that have accompanied the journey so far flow west to gain the Irish Sea via the River Mersey. The dmu is now heading along a short valley towards what seems to be a vertical wall of moorland, high up on which is the castellated ventilation shaft of the tunnel we are about to enter. It is an uphill grind to Cowburn with the entrance, soon to be seen ahead, offering no respite, for the gradient continues at 1 in 150 for just over a mile and a half along the tunnel's 3,702 yards, at which point the summit of the line is reached.

The work of building this tunnel proceeded in both directions from the bottom of the single shaft (one of the deepest in Britain) as well as from the other ends. When the headings met they were within one inch of lining up, which is a measure of late 19th century engineering skills. Indeed, the whole of this 20-mile section between Chinley North Junction and Dore, completed in 1894 to make a link between the Derby-Manchester and Derby-Sheffield main lines, forms a tribute to the development of the railway builders' art.

The scene, after leaving the short cutting at the end of the tunnel, is quite breathtaking. Ahead is a long, wide valley curving away out of sight at its far eastern end. To the right (south) the massive flank of Rushup Edge tapers to the hump of Mam Tor, followed by the gritty face of Back Tor and the superb, conical Lose Hill. These form a narrow sliver of hills jutting eastward from the previously mentioned saddle, creating the Vale of Edale, our present viewpoint, and the westward end of Hopedale to be seen later. From this point rivers and streams flow east and south to find, eventually, the North Sea. For the first half mile out of the tunnel the northern foreground is dominated by the great bulk of Grinslow Knoll forming the western flank of Grindsbrook which is now coming into view.

Grindsbrook! Well named is this stiff opening climb to the Pennine Way. The sight of a church tower pinpoints the location of the village of Edale (perhaps the most famous name in the rucksack world) standing four square across the open end of this gigantic fissure, for Grindsbrook is hardly a valley. From the train window you have the impression it ends against a black towering wall of rock, but in fact the brook takes a sharp westward turn before ascending steeply to the plateau.

Sometimes on a steeply graded line there is one place or section in particular where the gradient is clearly evident against the background topography. On the Hope Valley line this happens on the section between Edale and Hope stations. The sensation of descending, as the rails run east and then follow the valley shape in a long gradual curve south, is quite uncanny. Hillsides seem to become higher. Lose Hill appeared almost at eye level as the train emerged from the tunnel, but now it rises above like a Matterhorn in miniature as the line curves through 90 degrees around the lower flanks.

Hope station is now reduced to the status of a halt, but step backward in time and see its importance increase. In the pre-motor age intrepid 19th century travellers alighted here for Castleton, for various underground caverns and that delight of our Victorian and Edwardian forebears 'viewing the scenery'. However, there is not, as yet, need to abandon Hope, for those who enter here will even find a bus/rail connecting service, and how many small country stations can boast the facility today?

Beyond Hope look north-east to where the long slab side of Win Hill slopes up to a rocky knob (some fanciful folk still see this as the remains of an extinct

Above right: The Hope Valley line saw some of BR's last regular steam workings. Indeed, the 19.05 Earle's Sidings (west of Hope)-Widnes cement train was the final regular steam turn on the line. Here it is in the charge of LMS '8F' 2-8-0 No 48723 on 1 May 1968. / *L. A. Nixon*

Right: Present-day Hope Valley through train motive power, Class 40 No 40.117, passes Bamford with a Skegness-Manchester holiday working on 2 June 1978. / *A. R. Kaye*

volcano!). The great gap dividing this distinctive stony outcrop from the long gritty escarpment of Bamford Edge is the valley of the young Derwent River, the infant part of which now lies somewhere below the mighty Ladybower Reservoirs to the north.

A few hundred yards before Bamford, the next station, the Derwent is crossed by an iron girder bridge — the only one on the section. Here, as the Derwent joins the River Noe, our companion from Edale, so does the train enter the valley of one of the most beautiful waterways in the land. Hopedale is left behind as the ever growing Derwent begins a long southward sweep, eventually to pass across the parkland of Chatsworth, and then the broad lush beauty of Darley Dale to squeeze through the towering defile of the Matlocks.

For the railway traveller there are no more than a few glimpses of the Derwent in the magnificently wooded section between Hathersage, the next station, and Grindleford. The river is now set on its southward course but the way of the train is east.

Just a few hundred yards beyond the end of Grindleford station platforms is Totley, at 3 miles

950yds the longest land tunnel in Britain, and now waiting to swallow the train. The cutting which follows the tunnel is like a forest glade, which soon opens out into the picturesque outer suburbs of Sheffield, as we approach the station at Dore.

Dore stands astride a junction formed by the Manchester line and the main line to Derby and the south. It sees the passage of most of the North-East to South-West and St Pancras-Sheffield expresses; as well as the Manchester trains and the procession of freight services. The number of heavy, locomotive hauled trains to be seen, especially on a summer Saturday, is quite impressive. A fine spot, especially for anybody stirred by the sight of a big locomotive working hard, spectacular enough in steam days, but still a thrilling sight today. Watching a big diesel locomotive roaring away round the curve towards Bradway Tunnel is one of the high spots in present-day observation.

No intermediate stations remain between Dore and Sheffield, though in some cases evidence of their existence can be seen. The platform faces at Millhouses are still in situ, as is the shell of the old motive power depot, though it now encloses a different activity than ministering to the needs of steam locomotives. The old four-track layout has been considerably modified as a result of resignalling, lengthy portions now being two-track only, these sometimes veering slightly away from the old alignment, when perhaps the width of the old track bed can allow for improvements.

I have vivid recollections of this section in the days when the Chinley or Manchester 'stopper' would occasionally pace an express up the hill. I remember in particular one day in 1947 when I was passenger in the first coach behind a Midland Class '2' 4-4-0. I had settled down at Sheffield to enjoy the leisurely and private perambulation through green valleys as few passengers used it as a through route, so invariably one had the luxury of an empty compartment. Then I noticed that a 'Jubilee' had arrived at the up main line platform at Sheffield Midland and was lazily belching a frothy mixture of steam and smoke against the massive stone retaining wall. Perhaps there would be a

Left: **Illustrating the line's attraction as a steam route, the restored 'Royal Scot'** *Scots Guardsman* **storms up the bank to Cowburn Tunnel with the 'Yorkshire Venturer' charter train of 11 November 1978.** / *David Eatwell*
Below: The Eastern Region gained control of ex-LMS sheds in Sheffield in the late 1950s which then were allocated LNER locomotives. These worked trains such as the 16.31 Sheffield (Midland)-Chinley stopper with which 'B1' No 61093 drifts into Hope on 20 July 1963.
/ *Brian Stephenson*

chance of real excitement, though it would depend on smart platform work, for we were about to depart.

There was a sudden impression of urgency on the platform, with close scrutiny being given to the double chained timepiece held in the open palm. Then at the given moment, the elderly 4-4-0 slowly, painfully, prised itself away from Sheffield's platforms and gruffly 'whoof-pause-whoofed' away from the platform and through the short tunnel outside. Both engines had about $5\frac{1}{2}$ miles of 1 in 100 uphill, and for the 'Jubilee' there would be no respite until it reached the far end of Bradway Tunnel.

Despite the gradient the 4-4-0 was soon into an easy lolloping stride, and the deep-throated, hoarse voice from the chimney was set off by the front carriage coupling squeaking and lunging as if in a tug-of-war with the engine. A short pause at Heeley, the first station out, where a glance through the open window showed a distant column of smoke and steam. Already the echoes were being roused by a hard working 'Jubilee'. The express was still over a quarter of a mile away but thanks to our short pause the gap was beginning to narrow. However, judging by the exhaust from the toiling 4-6-0, the train on his tail must be heavy, so perhaps there was just a chance for the smaller engine to arrive at Dore first. After the few seconds pause we were flagged away, and with a shuddering roar the driving wheels commenced to spin. Then engine and driver, sensing competition,

quickly came to grips and we huff-puffed away, the seven-foot diameter driving wheels turning with that deceptively slow ease which was a characteristic of these engines.

The 4-4-0 had hardly begun to get a grip when it was necessary for another pause, this time at Millhouses. Meanwhile the 'Jubilee' crept nearer. Away again with deep, more purposeful huff, but it was too late. Before we had reached the platform ends there was a syncopated fanfare, a flurry of pungent smoke and steam and a rat-a-tat-tat of carriage bogies — 13 in all. With triumphant cry *Gilbert and Ellice Islands* — superb name — swept through on the fast line. The side view across a couple of platforms of that most elegant of locomotives, still in crimson lake livery, taking a firm grip on a heavy train is still very clear in the mind's eye.

The Class '2' lumbered on, the distance between the two gradually widening, and as we slowed down for Dore I could see the tail end of the express swaying round the curve towards Bradway Tunnel.

But we must return to Sheffield Midland, the end of our journey today just as it would have been 20 or 30 years ago. A journey of memories, from the steam-sizzling warmth of a winter's evening snuggled in an ancient LMS corridor, to the more spartan comfort of a dmu today.

Within the compass of 40 miles you will have discovered a unique blend of mill chimneys, mountain panorama, and lush green valley, a microcosm of the English north country scene. I believe this railway shows it to greater advantage than any other I know. But I would advise the intending traveller — take a leisurely view, use the local to New Mills, then the ramblers' train through the dales to Sheffield. For the journey along the Hope Valley line is one to be savoured with unhurried pleasure.

Above: The route's outwardly undistinguished principal train, the Harwich (Parkeston Quay)-Manchester boat train, drones westward behind 46.033 through Hope station on 18 February 1978. / L. A. Nixon

Below: Successor to the Midland 4-4-0s on the line's stopping trains, Ivatt '2' 2-6-0 No 46485 pulls away from Dore & Totley station with the 09.39 Sheffield-Chinley on 20 August 1966. / D. Booth

Footplating a DB 2-10-0

ROBIN RUSSELL

The announcement of the closure of Ottbergen shed during the summer of 1976 probably meant very little to most railway enthusiasts. Certainly this West German town, approximately 50 miles south of Hannover, was unknown to me until the autumn of the previous year. At this time Deutsche Bundesbahn had terminated a lengthy correspondence by issuing me with a pass to ride the locomotive of the 14.35 express freight from Ottbergen to Herzberg, returning after dark on the 19.49 departure.

I duly arrived in Ottbergen on 19 September 1975, DB having shown courtesy and efficiency in issuing me with a full set of documents including a rail ticket (first class, no less) for the round trip. I reported to Herr Kleibrink, an officer of the locomotive department who was to accompany me, and then met Driver (Lokomotivführer) Saake and Fireman (Heizer) Laaser. We made our way to the through station road

and awaited the arrival of train Dg 53849 from Altenbeken. This appeared behind three-cylinder 2-10-0 No 044 277-2, and consisted of mixed wagons totalling 1,022 tonnes. The crew changed over while water was taken; it was interesting to note that the British type of flexible water bag was not used: the filler pipe swung across and discharged vertically downwards into a large filling point at the rear of the tender.

I climbed into the cab of No 277-2 and took a look at the layout, observing that the fireman's controls were all on his (left) side, as was a giant mechanical

Above: Having arrived at Ottbergen, and before the author started his footplate trip, the 2-10-0 takes water. Note the water column.

Below: The driver's view from the footplate — a shot on the outward trip to Herzberg.

Right: Running downhill on a lengthy freight, sister engine No 044 326-7 makes a fine sight.

lubricator serving a multitude of feed pipes. The regulator moved across in GWR/LMS style but had to be pushed away from the driver to open. Nearby was a useful fixture for holding the day's train orders, illuminated (in common with all the gauges) by electric light.

As we waited for the signal to clear, Driver Saake operated the cylinder cocks and cracked open the regulator, sending a cloud of steam up in front of the engine. Not speaking German, by a puzzled frown I indicated the question 'why?'. The driver pointed to the pressure gauge, the needle hovering just below blowing-off point (16 bars, or 230lb/sq in). In turn I pointed towards the safety valves — surely they functioned correctly. He put his hands to his ears and waved towards an estate of houses nearby. Not a word spoken, but I clearly understood that steam was being released from the cylinders to avoid the noise of the safety valves popping. This was new to me, as previously I had seen blowing-off prevented by separate or combined use of dampers, injectors, fire door or additional fuel.

We were given the road three minutes late, leaving Ottbergen at 14.38. Before long the train was sending up echoes from the steelwork as we rumbled over the Weser river bridge. Here I was reminded of the Pied Piper of Hamelin: '.... until they came to the River Weser, wherein all plunged and perished!' The line then turned south, then east again, all the while following the river, which swung away from us until we saw it again at Bodenfelde. Here we suffered a one-minute stop for signals at 15.08. Until now, the engine had not been worked very hard, despite an 0.47% grade from km Post 20.5 up to Bodenfelde. Right from the re-start, however, I was to be left in no doubt as to the capability of engine and crew. Running alongside a tributary of the Weser, we headed through pleasant countryside as the 2-10-0 accelerated its heavy train. With full regulator and 30% cut-off we stormed past Vernawahlshausen, increasing to 35% at Uslar. Here the line swings sharply to the right and I looked back at our long train and the trail of black smoke. If there was one place I'd rather have been than on the footplate, it would have been by the lineside to record on tape and film the progress of the express freight.

At one point, the crew seemed very anxious for me to be on the left-hand side of the cab. Moving across, I saw sister engine No 044 326-7 speeding towards us, running downhill with another long goods train. We continued to climb, with controls unaltered. Boiler pressure was steady, just below blowing-off point, with steam-chest pressure only a little less — at this power output, a great tribute to the design of the steam passages.

We passed Volpriehausen, at 15.44, nearing the end of the long grade of 1.17% and 1.04%, with speed increasing but water falling in the glass. With the climb almost over, would the water level fall too far? Closing the regulator would cause a drop, as would the forward tilting of the engine as the down grade commenced. Moments later I realised that injector and/or feed pump were in action, for the level was well up before we entered the summit tunnel at Ertinghausen, the time being 15.51 as we passed km Post 46, just beyond the far portal.

From here there was a long downhill stretch, 044 277-2 running effortlessly at the maximum permitted speed of 50mile/h. Track and locomotive must have been in superb condition, as the ride was so smooth that I was able to make very legible notes while standing on one foot.

It was interesting to note the method of locomotive working under this near-coasting condition. The reverser was in full-forward gear and the regulator was cracked. I recalled the consternation of the BR loco chiefs, soon after nationalisation, on discovering the wide disparity between the coasting procedures on the various regions.

We passed over the tracks from Gottingen, then running alongside these until we headed slowly through the junction station at Northeim (40 miles and 89min from Ottbergen) at 16.07, bearing right from the main line north to Hannover.

The remaining 17 miles to our destination were unremarkable, although the locomotive had to be opened up to climb grades of 0.5% to 0.9% for the final six miles to Herzberg, reached at 16.51 — still three minutes late. No 044 277-2 was detached from its train for the tender first run, light, back to Northeim for servicing. Coal and water were replenished, the engine turned and the fire cleaned. This process was very interesting, being far removed from the usual half-hearted removal of the bigger pieces of clinker.

First of all, the drop-gate was wound down. Then some 90% of the fire was raked through the dropped area. When the grate was almost cleared, the drop portion was wound up again and some coal spread over the small fire still remaining. Even when we started back towards Herzberg, the grate was barely covered with burning coal. On this short run, as dusk was falling, I noted that 30% cut-off with 100lb in the steam chest took us up the bank to Herzberg yards.

For the return, on train Dg 53848, we had a lighter load of 860 tonnes. Leaving Herzberg four minutes late at 19.53, we were barely under way before the train was rolling down the hill towards Northeim, passed at 20.22. Next came the really interesting part of the westbound journey, the climb to Ertinghausen Tunnel. With the lighter train 30% cut-off sufficed, the regulator being not fully open, boiler pressure 210lb and with 190lb in the steam chest. Even compared with the outward trip, this was a great experience. As we blasted our way through the night, the bark of the exhaust could be heard both from the chimney and through the fire door. The green of the signals rushed up out of the darkness, while in the cab the electrically-lit gauges were supplemented by the glare from the fire.

The firing technique used on the 2-10-0 was of

interest. DB shovels were large, probably even longer than the GWR pattern. Fireman Laaser used a deceptively casual swing for the easier spells, but when maximum steam production was required the coal was despatched with speed and rhythm. Unique, certainly to my knowledge, was the fireman's use of a hat with a peak made of welding-goggle material. I had a look through this and found that the state of the firebed could be clearly seen even at full output. A power-operated firedoor would have found good use at the hands of this engine crew, who combined to keep the door closed whenever possible. At high outputs when prolonged door opening would have admitted too much secondary air (not to mention scorching the fireman's legs), the driver would often operate the door. This was far larger than on any BR class and was hinged at the top, counter-balanced and swinging outward (back) to open. The precise timing, with the driver's left hand moving the counterweight whenever a shovelful of coal was on the way, was indicative of the coordination between these two very professional footplatemen.

Entering Ertinghausen Tunnel the remainder of the trip was now over favourable grades. Due to pass Lauenforde at 21.28, in the event we were stopped for signals between 21.28 and 21.37, to allow an eastbound train to come off the single track section. We pulled into Ottbergen at 21.54, 13 minutes late.

This memorable day left me with a very high regard for West German steam locomotive operation while a feature of the two runs had been the great hospitality which fully overcame the seemingly immense language barrier.

All of which brings me back to the beginning, with my application for permission to ride an '044'. This class had always interested me, not only for their performance in the 1970s, but also for the advanced design features which were introduced in the 1920s. For example, the UK had to wait for Bulleid in 1941 before an entire class appeared with electric lighting and with all the fireman's controls grouped on one side of the cab. However, the Southern's 'Last Giant of Steam' (and the greatest) might well have reflected on the cool cabs of the '044s' resulting from the external location of the steam manifold. Also, many British classes would have benefited from the provision of compensated springing, which in the case of the '044s' was divided into one group for the front four axles and another for the rear two.

On the production side, the class was built to what were then very advanced principles of interchangeable manufacture. Various engines were converted to burn oil and also coal dust and mechanical stokers were fitted to some. While there have been dimensional differences between batches, the table gives data which are typical.

Besides my indebtedness to DB, for help with communications and translation, my thanks also go to Elizabeth and Gaby, while invaluable technical advice was received from A. F. C. Morris, R. T. Price and world steam authority A. E. Durrant.

Below: Portrait of a fine locomotive type. No 044 277-2 eases into Ottbergen, to a crew change and water stop.

Dimensions of the DB '044' 2-10-0s

Introduced	Cylinders (3)	Driving wheels (diameter)	Boiler pressure	Tractive effort (85% boiler pressure)	Grate area	Piston valves	Valve gear	Firebox	Heating surface	Locomotive weight
1926	21.7in dia × 26in stroke	4ft 7in	230lb sq in	64,000lb	51sq ft	11.8in diameter	Heusinger (German equivalent of Walschaert)	Round-top Wide grate	2.550sq ft	112 tons

For the love of steam –Easter '78

DAVID EATWELL

It all began, I suppose, way back in the winter of 1977 when the list of the main-line steam tours for 1978 was published, and when the rumour that the Settle and Carlisle was to see steam at Easter after a gap of almost 10 years was confirmed. *Green Arrow* over Ais Gill! The thought of such an exciting prospect filled us

Good Friday, 24 March. Above (1): *Owain Glyndwr* **(left) and** *Prince of Wales* **(right) being prepared for their duties on Aberystwyth shed.** *Owain Glyndwr*, **No 7, had recently been converted to oil-firing — note some of the associated pipework on front of the cab.** *Prince of Wales*, **No 9, was still a coal burner and No 8,** *Llewellyn*, **was away at Swindon.** / *All photos by the author*

Left (2): The second train of the day was worked by No 9. Only a superhuman effort enabled us to reach the spot to photograph her. No 7 on the first train had had to stop for a blow-up, the oil-firing perhaps not yet being properly adjusted. Below (3): Later in the day No 7 worked back to Aberystwyth with the stock of the second train and is seen here near Capel Bangor.

all with keen anticipation, and immediately we started formulating plans to witness the event. Unfortunately, the best laid plans, etc, and with only two weeks to the off, I was suddenly summoned to go into hospital for an operation to relieve the sinusitus from which I had been suffering (and I do mean suffering) for some time, and I was discharged — with a new nose! — just five days before we were due to leave.

As in previous years, our first day away — Good Friday — was to be spent on the Vale of Rheidol, but since I was convalescent, the possibility of driving some 2,500 miles in little more than $3\frac{1}{2}$ days seemed behaviour hardly conducive to a speedy recovery; so alternate plans had to be brought into force, and instead of doing my usual marathon stint at the wheel, I found myself promoted to the exalted position of navigator for the whole weekend.

And so, come seven o'clock on Good Friday morning, Big John in his Escort arrived at my house in Bedford, having collected Wilf on the way, and the

Easter Saturday. Above (4): Yes, I know it's a hackneyed view but none of us had done it before. Just before the loco emerged into the open, the regulator was closed and a wonderful smoke display disappeared in an instant.

Bottom right (5): No 60009 had left its home at Markinch at 08.19 to run light to Edinburgh for its 09.52 departure with the Aberdeen special. Here we enjoyed seeing it pass early morning golfers near the Fife Coast at Burntisland.

Easter Sunday. Below (6): A thaw had well and truly set in by the time any of us had woken up at 10 o'clock this morning. While we were pitching our tents some eight hours previously in this Beattock lay-by, the snow was settling heavily and it needed real determination to put the tents up at all! Big John is admiring the scene from the left-hand tent; Pete is doing the same from the other one. Wilf is wandering around, no doubt wishing that we would all get up and get off to a restaurant for a hot meal.

Easter Sunday. Right (7): On the Lakeside & Haverthwaite Railway, a lunchtime train from Haverthwaite nears Windermere (Lakeside). The locos are *Cumbria*, a Hunslet 0-6-0ST, works No 3698 of 1950, ex-NCB Ladysmith and *Repulse*, ex-MoD, a similar locomotive, works No 3794 of 1953. The latter is making one of its first outings after major repairs. It is probably the only preserved locomotive in the UK with a Giesl ejector.

three of us set off for Aberystwyth. We arrived there soon after noon, depositing Wilf at the station as he wanted to catch the 13.30 train to Devils Bridge while Big John and I photographed from the lineside. First we inspected the locos 'on shed' (1), and then set off up the line, aided by the relevant OS map. With some sadness, we noted that oil-firing had deprived *Owain Glyndwr* not only of his 'bark', but also of much of the characteristic 'clag' that had made these locomotives so spectacular a sight when working hard against the grade. Fortunately, at the time of our visit, *Prince of Wales* had still to succumb and, at the head of the 14.10 train (2), did not disappoint us with his audio-visual display. We photographed both downward trains (3) as far as we could, while Wilf returned on the second one in order to 'do' both locos, and after collecting him back in Aberystwyth, we all set off on the next leg of the journey.

Our first port of call was Llanfair — Big John is a member, and would never have considered passing without making at least a brief courtesy-call on his beloved *Earl* and *Countess*, where *Joan* was still in steam after making three trips to Sylfaen earlier in the

day. Then it was Oswestry for a bite to eat and to try to see the 'Cambrian' locos — *Foxcote Manor* etc — but this once important railway centre had declined so severely of recent years that we felt we would linger no longer than was really necessary. We set off for Leek in Staffordshire where we were to meet Pete from Daventry and transfer to the much more luxurious surroundings of his fine 1800. The Escort was left at the house of some relatives of mine for safe keeping, and Pete who, unlike us, had been at work all that day, sped us through the night to Edinburgh, with but a brief stop for sleep in the car somewhere near Penicuik.

How attractive big cities can be early in the morning, and particularly Edinburgh at 06.00 with the air filled with the aroma of baking bread, the attractive stone buildings and the wide thoroughfares empty, except for the occasional newspaper-boy (or girl!), and given a bygone atmosphere by the horse-drawn milk-

floats; something that those of us from the south will only have seen before if we're old enough!

The reason for a journey this far north was, of course, *Union of South Africa* which Wilf wanted to travel behind, and which the rest of us wished to chase. After leaving Wilf at Waverley, Big John, Pete and I crossed the Forth and prepared for the day's photography along the line to Aberdeen. Since all of us had been up here before, we were fairly familiar with the route, but light engine movements were new to us, and we were lucky to catch No 60009 in the early morning sunshine (5), before a howling gale rolled in the clouds . These conditions lasted all day (4), and were on occasion something of an embarrassment, since the exhaust from the loco was blown down on to the train, almost completely obscuring it from view . All in all, though, it was a most successful day photographically, due in no small part to Pete at the wheel, doing a great job in getting us from 'phot-spot'

to 'phot-spot' safely, and in the minimum time possible.

At the end of the trip, and with Wilf back on board again, we set off southwards towards our overnight stopping-place (6), and for an easy day on the two steam lines in the Lake District. The Lakeside and Haverthwaite Railway provided us with our first set of pictures (7), and the Ravenglass and Eskdale Railway our second set (8)(9). A lot of these seemed to feature Wilf near the front of the train as he made at least one journey on each line.

After a second really rough night in a row, Easter Monday dawned bright and clear as we greeted the day through the flaps of our tents. Using Big John's OS maps, I got down to the task of navigating Pete over the Settle and Carlisle in such a way as to take maximum advantage of the stops made by *Green Arrow*, and I'm happy to say that despite the dull weather later in the day, it will long remain one of the highlights of my life as a steam enthusiast. Personally,

I have rarely been so moved by any sight as I was when No 4771 burst out from under the bridge at Ais Gill (11) — the nearest perhaps was when the last '012' Pacific ran up to Emden. On the latter occasion it was pure pathos, but this was absolute elation and as the majestic procession passed us with Bill Harvey waving regally from 'his' footplate, I'll swear that I was not the only one to cheer and wave back! Even now, all this time later, despite having thrilled to the sights and sounds of *Flying Scotsman*, *Evening Star*, *Clan Line* and *Sir Nigel Gresley* all doing the same thing — some of them more than once — and

Easter Sunday. Ravenglass & Eskdale Railway. Above (8): *River Esk* arrives at Irton Road in dismal weather in the mid-afternoon. During 1978 I made about a dozen visits to the area taking some 150 photographs of steam and only saw sun and steam in concert some two or three times. Left: (9): For just about 2 seconds, the sun came out when *Northern Rock* was on Dalegarth turntable.

Easter Monday.
Above right (10): While steam was having its final fling on the lines to Carlisle in the late 1960s, this neck of the woods was somewhat inaccessible to me, so before this occasion I had never seen steam on the Settle & Carlisle. But here it is, bathed in sunshine. As so often happens, though, the regulator was closed just before *Green Arrow* reached us. A pity, since we had spent most of the morning finding a fairly secluded scenic spot, beside an uphill stretch of line and where the light was right. This is near Lazonby.

Right: Some snow is lying on Wild Boar Fell (background) as the special reaches Ais Gill summit. Two days earlier, photographers here had to contend with a blizzard on *Green Arrow*'s trip north. Although we were latecomers to the spot we were able — just — to squeeze in among the hundreds of other photographers already there.

the anticipation of, perhaps, 'Jubilees', 'Black Fives', and maybe others, following in the footsteps of their predecessors in succeeding years, nothing could ever detract from that first experience, and I shall quite happily take the memory of No 4771 with me to the grave (11).

Our last sight of 'The Norfolkman' was as it pulled away from Settle, and then we joined the queue of homebound caravans on the A65, travelling nose-to-tail at up to 10mile/h. At the first opportunity we peeled off to the south towards Preston, the M6, and Leek to change cars for the last leg homewards, and to reflect on an unforgettable weekend which by no stretch of the imagination could be described as incident-free! I won't dwell on the biggest disaster of all, which was when we were waiting at the south end of the Tay Bridge, cameras all set up, only to see *Union of South Africa* take the train on its usual route along the north bank towards Perth (12), but instead mention the time near Stonehaven when, after photographing the 'A4', we ran back to the car to find that while it had been sitting stationary in a car-park, some joker had run into the back of it and bent its bumper. There was another vexing moment at Ravenglass when we returned from a conducted tour of the shed to discover a flat tyre . . . and the jack was in Daventry! Our thanks to the signalman who lent us his, thank goodness. Among the 'celebrities' we

encountered was Pat Phoenix (Elsie Tanner of Coronation Street) having breakfast in the Granada Service Area at Southwaite near Carlisle, sitting at a table near us as we downed coffee after a cold night's camping. She left before us though; Big John thought she might have been fed up with all the people who kept coming up and asking her if that was really David Eatwell over there! We also had the experience — at 11 o'clock on Easter Sunday night — of a police escort through Carlisle to the hospital after Big John collapsed in a dead faint while we were putting up the tents, with the embarrassment of having him recover before we reached there! And the worry right at the end when he discovered the loss of his wallet. It wasn't the money so much as his Welshpool membership card going astray that upset him. But a few days later, a letter arrived from Armathwaite with the news that the wallet had been found just where he had collapsed, and the membership card was still inside. He *was* relieved.

On Thursday of the same week I went (overnight) with Robin (of the Quainton Road Society) to spend a day at Pontardulais for the last time before steam finished at Craig Merthyr colliery. The next day I left with Pete (in his 1800 again) for France and the 230G special between Paris and Rouen, sleeping this time in the car. We had a car-full, too: accompanying us were Alan (from the Nene Valley Railway), John and his

Flashback to my biggest photographic misdemeanour. Having directed my companions to the wrong end of the Tay Bridge we then made an almighty dash across Northern Fife and arrived at this level crossing outside Auchterarder. I was the only one able to get out of the car quick enough for this shot over the gate Left (12).

Above: 30 March 1978. About 08.00, 0-6-0ST Bagnall No 2758 of 1944 takes water at Craig Merthyr after bringing up a train of empties from Pontardulais.

Below: 2 April 1978. Just a few days later I was in France, seeing this preserved Paris Orleans 4-6-0 No 230.G.353 working a Paris-Rouen special, and stopping here at Evreux.

younger brother Peter from London, and Pete's young son Ian. Returning home at about four on Monday morning (the car had run out of petrol in Calais, and we had to push it the last half mile or so on to the ferry, and then get it towed off at Dover; shame, shame!), I attended the out-patients clinic that afternoon and was declared fit to go back to work next day . . . but only just!!

And then some people say that photographers have it all their own way! Even so, we are eternally grateful to the owners and operators of steam locomotives for giving us some marvellous spectacles, knowing just how much work goes into it all. But without photographers, and publishers printing our work, perhaps there would be less people to fill the trains in the first place.

Woodhead, no more?

R. C. LOW and J. S. WHITELEY

Above: To British eyes in the 1950s this sort of scene epitomised the promise of the Woodhead electrified route. Class EM2 Co-Co No 27003 passes Penistone at speed on the Liverpool-Harwich boat train on 26 February 1955. / Kenneth Field

It is still possible to see locomotives, the design of which can be traced back to Sir Nigel Gresley's era, in regular service on British Rail. It is also possible to witness the sight of four locomotives doing battle with one of the steepest gradients on a main line in Britain; on a line blessed with more than its fair share of spectacular scenery, graceful viaducts and a rather long tunnel. In short, this is an introduction to the Manchester-Sheffield-Wath lines.

The recent speculation over the line's future adds just one more sad chapter to a story of disappointment and delay which would justify a subtitle to this article of the 'Too Late Train'.

Although Lancashire had, and has, a coalfield of its own, industry in the County Palatine always demanded fuel of a quantity and quality in excess of local production, and railway companies were not slow in realising the potential of Yorkshire-Lancashire coal traffic. Yorkshire has always been a net exporter of coal and trains travelled to the four points of the compass from the South Yorkshire area.

The principal parts in the trans-Pennine theatre were played by the Lancashire and Yorkshire, the Midland and the Great Central, the latter being blessed with the shortest route from the coalfield to

Manchester's conurbation. Unfortunately, the Pennines provided an unwelcome barrier. Over the years, big steam power was the order of the day on all lines except the Midland, and the hills echoed to the sound of eight-coupled goods engines from the turn of the century.

On the Great Central, 0-8-0s gave way to the famous Robinson 2-8-0s or 'Tinies', latterly known as '04s', and these were often worked in pairs. Even this combination did not cope with the shocking $3\frac{1}{2}$ miles at 1 in 40 of Worsborough bank and several more locomotives were frequently to be found at the back of a train helping it up to Barnsley Junction, Penistone. Electrification of the line appealed to the Great Central at about the time of World War I but nothing was

done about it. So, shortly after taking office with the newly-formed LNER, Gresley introduced the solitary Garratt in 1925 to assist in banking trains up Worsborough incline. There is no doubt, however, that electrification was still in the minds of the powers that be. By the early 1930s, the traffic may have passed its peak, but it was still enormously heavy and the line was expensive and difficult to operate. In LNER terms, it was important, being the railway's only link between Manchester (and Liverpool via the Cheshire Lines Committee lines) and London, and it must have been a nightmare trying to provide paths for swift expresses in between the slow coal hauls.

When the Government offered railway companies long-term, low interest rate loans for capital investment in the mid-1930s, the LNER was at last presented with an opportunity to realise its ambitions and electrification was authorised in 1936. C. Hamilton Ellis, writing in the RCTS *Locomotive Stock Journal* published in 1937, recommended a few names for locomotives 'when the Manchester-Sheffield business is completed'. One of Hamilton Ellis's suggestions — *Electra* — was actually used, but he could not have guessed that 22 years would elapse before naming would take place.

Gresley, as Chief Mechanical Engineer on the LNER, had a direct hand in the design of the prototype Manchester-Sheffield electric locomotive, No 6701, which was outshopped in 1941, the year of Gresley's untimely death. Other work already undertaken included detailed planning for all lines to be electrified and the erection along many miles of masts to support the overhead wires. In addition to the lines which are now electrified, there were plans to extend the overhead on to the CLC into Manchester Central and the industrial complex of Trafford Park.

However, despite all this progress, the project had to be shelved due to the war, and there are numerous photographs in existence of woebegone Great Central 4-6-0s and 2-8-0s wheezing along between rows of impressive but useless overhead masts. Another significant fact is that these masts led right up to the mouths of the old Woodhead tunnels.

After the war, the project recommenced against the discouraging news that the Woodhead tunnels were becoming more and more troublesome while No 6701, which had spent the war pottering about the jointly-owned Manchester, South Junction and Altrincham line, went off to Holland to help the Dutch in their postwar recovery. But as an additional benefit, the locomotive would get some proper main line use so that the design could be thoroughly tested.

After years of diverting traffic, due to the closure of first one bore, and then the other, in an attempt to restore the Woodhead tunnels to a fit condition, the newly formed Railway Executive threw in the towel

and authorised the building of a new tunnel on 15 November 1948 due to 'the age, condition, high maintenance costs and restricted profile prohibiting the erection of overhead wires'. The latter point seems surprising in view of the obvious plan previously to electrify the old tunnels. Perhaps 6701 and her sisters would have stuck fast or, even worse, electrocuted themselves in the old bore on opening day, much to the chagrin of the LNER directorate, had not the war intervened and the Railway Executive assumed responsibility!

The decision to build a new tunnel came after the plan to complete electrification and, therefore, the displacement of steam locomotives took place in stages over a very much longer period than had been originally hoped. Furthermore, the tunnel took a long time to build and was not completed until late in 1953. Meanwhile, the Dutch Railways, although duly grateful for a loan of our locomotive, christening it *Tommy* along the way, had found that it had a very small cab and gave just about as rough a ride as could be imagined!

Largely as a result of their observations, various modifications were made to give the crews more room and a better driving position, while the original order for 65 Bo-Bos was trimmed to 58, and a new design of passenger locomotive with non-articulated six-wheeled bogies was developed, to cope with passenger trains running at higher speeds.

Electrification could not wait for the dilatory tunnel and so by the end of 1951 the first 30 Bo-Bos were exercised on driver training duties by piloting trans-Pennine freights from Wath to Worsborough. Stage 1 of the electrification was inaugurated officially on 4 February 1952, when all freight between Wath and

Opposite page: The EM1 Bo-Bos in their early days. Top: Two locomotives, the leading one No 26007, stand at Ilford car depot in February 1951 when undergoing trials on Great Eastern territory. / J. F. Aylard

Centre: Nos 26039/42 pass Worsborough Bridge, on the Penistone-Wath section, with a Lowton St Mary's-Barnby Dun freight in June 1955. / P. J. Lynch

Bottom: In June 1954 three Bo-Bos pause for breath at Penistone exchange sidings. / J. W. Armstrong

EM2 heyday. Above: Very smartly turned out, No 27000 poses on the Gorton-Reddish spur with a conference delegates' special, to allow the passengers to inspect Gorton sub-station. / Dr E. M. Patterson

Below: In November 1954 the 09.43 Cleethorpes-Manchester express, complete with restaurant car, nears Godley behind No 27003. / B. K. B. Green

Dunford Bridge became electrically hauled. This date was timely because, on 1 February, the LNER's Garratt, by now numbered 69999, disgraced itself by failing when banking a coal train up the incline. It was reported as having been withdrawn on the spot but, as is well known, survived a few more years, converted to burn oil, and, for a second time, was to compete with the Midland 0-10-0 No 58100 on its home territory in the Lickey Hills.

Stage 2 of electrification was to be the Manchester-Hadfield section, together with the branches, and the third stage was to complete the exercise by energising the Hadfield-Dunford Bridge line (through the tunnel) and the Penistone-Rotherwood Exchange sidings route, thus enabling the passenger services to be electrically hauled. With nationalisation, the link over to Manchester Central had become unnecessary and was not therefore electrified.

In the event, these plans were altered, and Stage 2 included all lines west of Dunford Bridge including the multiple unit operated Manchester-Glossop-Hadfield line and the various spurs towards such places as Stalybridge and Ashton Moss. This stage of electrification was inaugurated on 14 June 1954, although for some months previously recent deliveries of Bo-Bos had been piloting eastbound freights from Godley Junction, near Manchester, to Crowden, high up on the Pennines, for driver training. 'Piloting' is not quite the right word, as with their regulators shut the 2-8-0s ignominiously fizzled along behind the electrics. Having reached Crowden, the Bo-Bos then bounced back down to the Manchester area light engine to show off again on the next available eastbound freight. Prior to 14 June 1954, through passenger trains were still steam hauled, though the Great Central 4-6-0s had by now given way to the ubiquitous 'B1s'.

When Stage 2 was inaugurated, every main line train west of Penistone was turned over to electric haulage and Penistone became the changeover point for steam haulage to and from Sheffield. But this was to be shortlived as Stage 3, Penistone to Sheffield Victoria, was completed in September 1954 and steam all but disappeared when the short section from Victoria to Rotherwood Exchange sidings was energised at the beginning of 1955, Rotherwood becoming the changeover point for steam freights. Incidentally, the Penistone-Sheffield section included Thurgoland Tunnel which, being too small for the overhead wires, was reduced to take a single track and a new tunnel was built to take westbound traffic.

In a fit of enthusiasm between 1959 and 1961 the seven Co-Cos and the 12 Bo-Bos fitted with steam heating for use on passenger trains all received names. By now, however, the number of passenger trains had been reduced, with the withdrawal of the Marylebone-Manchester expresses, and with dieselisation the Harwich-Manchester train was turned over to through haulage by a Class 37 diesel. Surprisingly, the electric locomotives were given nameplates cast in authentic Great Central style, this being offset by the lined green livery that had by now replaced their original black paintwork. The enterprise was fairly shortlived for rationalisation of trans-Pennine services and the closure of Sheffield Victoria saw the through locomotive hauled passenger service withdrawn early in 1970. So the nameplates were removed shortly afterwards when the Co-Cos (Nos 27001-6) became surplus to requirements. As a nice touch of irony they were sold to our Dutch friends (probably after being assured that they rode very differently from old *Tommy*!). One of the writers was in Holland recently and saw a Co-Co at the head of a very different train from those for which it had originally been designed — an international express in Rotterdam Centraal station.

The 58 Bo-Bos have now been reduced in numbers to 38, reflecting the reduction in wagonload traffic, as most trans-Pennine coal, such as to Fiddlers Ferry power station, now moves in high-capacity, air-braked wagons. Track layouts, particularly the Glossop line, and marshalling yards have been reduced to a shadow of their former selves.

Much more could be said about the many unusual features of the line and its locomotives — particularly the latter's weight transfer feature to aid traction, Clearcall cab radio communication and, of course, the regenerative braking system. From the mid-1960s rationalisation of Woodhead line freight services had been accompanied by the running of heavier individual trains with the result that the Bo-Bos were equipped for multiple working. The need to increase the number of paths for such trains had been a major influence in pressing for withdrawal of the passenger trains, particularly as much freight traffic was transferred from other trans-Pennine routes.

Why should there be talk of closure of the Woodhead route? By the late 1970s a number of circumstances have conspired to make a major decision a certainty. Isolated electrification of a freight line depends upon the concentration of traffic at source and the dissipation of traffic at a centralised distribution point. In earlier days, freight trains were marshalled to work between major yards (rather than traffic destinations) and Wath and Mottram are good examples of such yards on the Woodhead route. From

Right: In October 1975 a Bo-Bo, now designated Class 76, passes Torside en route for Penistone with a freight.
/ J. Dowdeswell

Left: A Class 506 electric multiple unit crosses Dinting Viaduct on 8 September 1978. / *A. J. Booth*

Right: Before Stage 2 of the electrification was inaugurated, an ex-GC 'Tiny' 2-8-0 takes a train of empties eastwards near Godley East on 26 September 1953. / *N. Fields*

Below right: EM1 Bo-Bo No 26035 in the glory of its lined green livery with yellow painted roof. / *P. J. Sharpe*

Below: The Harwich-Manchester boat train had become the only through daytime express train over the Woodhead route by the late 1960s and had been turned over to diesel haulage, the Class 37 locomotive working out and back from Parkeston Quay. Not long before the train was diverted to the Hope Valley route, No 6723 leads its eight-coach train near Wortley on 22 November 1969. / *P. J. Rose*

Victorian days through to the mid-1960s, dozens of Yorkshire collieries were dispatching individual wagonloads of coal for a million households and thousands of industrial users all over the North-West. But we now live in the age of the block merry-go-round train of specialised fuel which goes direct from colliery to power station while industrial and domestic use of coal has been drastically reduced in favour of oil, gas and electric heating.

Traffic through marshalling yards in individual wagons has plummeted and visits to Wath today reveal the paucity of wagon humping and marshalling. With block train working of coal it really would be just as easy to retain the diesel at the head of the train for its trip over the Pennines until it reaches its destination in the North-West. The same applies to the other block, or company freight trains moving between Yorkshire and Lancashire, or Cheshire.

Also, the 1,500V dc electrification is non-standard and becoming life-expired. With 25kV ac electrification now the norm, and with thoughts of a major main-line electrification programme, BR must inevitably consider conversion of the Woodhead route to 25kV ac (but at £46m-odd that would be expensive) or, for reasons to be discussed, an undesirable conversion to diesel traction.

Undoubtedly, in spite of the comparatively new

Aspects of latter-day Woodhead route operation. Below: Nos 76.010/22 work back to Yorkshire as light engines — note the jumper cables for multiple working on the cab of 76.010. They have just emerged from Woodhead Tunnel. As most of the laden traffic is westbound, such light running is inevitable. Above: Benign in fair weather, Woodhead is normally a bleak spot. A westbound freight approaches Woodhead Tunnel. To the right are the portals of the old tunnels. / John S. Whiteley

Above right: On the Worsborough line 76.051 drops down the famous incline towards Wath to await a banking duty with the next westbound freight. / John S. Whiteley

Below right: The emus are still hard at work. This set, now designated Class 506, is seen soon after departure from Manchester Piccadilly, passing Ardwick. / B. Watkins

Woodhead Tunnel, it is a very expensive line to operate, with its massive earthworks and bridges, and, particularly at the eastern end, several manned level crossings. With definite indications that freight movements are reducing (the 30 or 40 daily departures from Wath reported in 1952 are rarely achieved today) it would not be unthinkable to re-route all trains by way of either the Hope Valley, L&Y Calder Valley or LNW Diggle trans-Pennine lines.

Lastly, Woodhead Tunnel was designed with electrification in mind and consequently has only one main ventilation shaft. The result is that dieselisation of the line would probably be unacceptable. Some time ago, Hope Valley line trains were routed round via the tunnel and were diesel hauled just to gauge the effect. Apparently, the interior of the tunnel became quite horrific, not to mention the constant pall of blue smoke pouring out of the mouth at Dunford Bridge.

It would be good to see the line converted to 25kV ac with restoration of the passenger service which would fit in very well with the Manchester Piccadilly scene, although re-routing of passenger trains would present problems at the Sheffield end, seeing that Midland station cannot easily be reached off the Woodhead route, and through connections are imperative. This sort of enterprise would provide opportunities for a cross-Manchester Altrincham to Hadfield suburban link but one fears that, instead, this section of the old Great Central will be allowed to wither and die, just like the London extension, with the freight traffic diverted to the alternative routes.

In that event, a modern electrified railway that the GCR and LNER both dreamed of, and a nationalised organisation brought into reality, will slide into limbo with nothing but the Hadfield/Glossop suburban trains (doubtless replaced by shabby diesel multiple units) to remind us of what once was. Even so, with the spectre of a fuel-hungry future, perhaps the authorities will look kindly at probably the best potential trans-Pennine route possessed by British Rail.

Branch line retrospect

In the twenty years since the massive closures of the late 1950s and early 1960s, miles of British railway have become no more than vague overgrown trails across the country. No more so than in Lincolnshire and the East Midlands.

The ex-GNR 'C12' 4-4-2Ts dominated certain branch lines. Left: A particular haunt was the Stamford East to Essendine branch. No 67357 leaves the terminus with the 07.33 for Essendine and the GN main line in 1956. Above: An evocative study of the same branch on 29 November 1949 with No 7368 taking the midday train out of Stamford. Below left: More than adequate power is provided by ex-GCR 'A5/1' 4-6-2T No 69803 for this 1954 Louth-Willoughby 'loop' train at Mablethorpe made up of an ex-GNR articulated set. Right: Some lines saw modern locomotives. Ivatt '4' 2-6-0 No 43082 at Braceborough Spa on the afternoon Bourne-Essendine freight of 7 April 1951. / *All photos by P. H. Wells*

Below: The Highdyke branch saw heavy ironstone traffic unitl the early 1970s. '02/3' 'Tango' 2-8-0 No 63936 approaches Colsterworth mine sidings with empties on 14 January 1951. Bottom: One of the last push-pull worked lines was the Seaton-Stamford 'shuttle'. On LNW metals now, Ivatt '2' 2-6-2T No 41219 has just passed Luffenham Junction for Seaton on 27 September 1965.

An ultimate steam locomotive design

C. P. ATKINS BSc

A 'Niagara' at speed along the NYC's magnificent 'Water Level Route' main line beside the Hudson River. The locomotive is No 6007. / *Cecil J. Allen Collection*

Above: The impressive ground level view of the Baker valve gear and Boxpok wheels of a 'Niagara'. Note the use of roller bearings.

Right: Looking newly ex-works is the first production 'S1b' No 6001 which was delivered in October 1945. / Cecil J. Allen Collection

If regarded purely as a traffic machine then the ultimate development of the conventional simple-expansion reciprocating steam locomotive was surely the New York Central 'Niagara' 4-8-4. Appearing at the eleventh hour of the steam era the class was the logical development of 275 4-6-4 passenger Hudsons and an even greater number of 4-8-2 fast freight Mohawks. The vast majority of both 4-6-4s and 4-8-2s were constructed by the American Locomotive Company (Alco) at Schenectady, NY, in close collaboration with Paul W. Kiefer, Chief Engineer Motive Power and Rolling Stock, New York Central System.

The first NYC 4-6-4 built in 1927 weighed 343,000lb and developed a maximum of 3,900ihp. The design was progressively developed and improved and when the last was delivered 11 years later, although weighing only 5% more, it developed 21.2% more maximum power (360,000lb and 4,725ihp). Although probably the best known, the NYC Hudsons were by no means the largest American 4-6-4s, but the final 'J3a' of 1937/8 represented the maximum practicable development of the type as far as the New York Central was concerned. By this time several major US railroads had made use of the larger 4-8-4 type for some years but the exceptionally level NYC main line

enabled Central to run 1,000-short ton trains made up of 15 air-conditioned passenger cars between Harmon, NY and Chicago behind its six-coupled Hudsons.

Nevertheless, by 1941 plans were being advanced for a 4-8-4 which would probably have appeared the following year but for the USA's involvement in World War II. This placed an immediate embargo on new locomotive design, but at last in April 1944 an order was placed with Alco for a solitary prototype for exhaustive testing. At a ceremony at the Schenectady plant the new locomotive was formally handed over to NYC officials on 10 March 1945. Thomas E. Dewey, then Governor of New York, was present.

Numbered 6000 on account of its nominal horsepower rating, the new 4-8-4 was officially dubbed 'combination passenger and freight locomotive' but rapidly became more familiarly known as a Niagara. Central's 4-8-4s were never Northerns, just as its 4-8-2s were never Mountains. The loading gauge being more restrictive in the east than in the west, the maximum permissible height was only 15ft 2¾in which only left room for an all but non-existent chimney 7in high. Surprisingly, the twin exhaust arrangement applied to a final batch of somewhat similar Alco 4-8-4s for the Union Pacific built in 1944 was not adopted. By the same token provision of a dome was a virtual impossibility and steam was collected via a slotted pipe in the steam space. The boiler was made as large as possible within the limitations, having a maximum outside diameter of 100in, which yielded a free gas area of 10.57sq ft, or 10½% of the grate area. It was mounted on a cast steel bed with cylinders integral and Timken roller bearings were applied to *all* axles and to *all* crank pins. Although by no means the largest of American 4-8-4s, maximum piston thrust could amount to 142,000lb and this was halved between the second and third coupled axles by means of tandem side rods. Also lateral motion devices allowed ⁵⁄₈in and ⁵⁄₁₆in lateral play to the first and second coupled axles respectively. Coupled with the latest balancing techniques this resulted in a very smooth riding locomotive, as was remarked upon by at least two British commentators. E. S. Cox was privileged to ride on No 6003 when brand new in October 1945 between Schenectady and Utica, as he described in his *Locomotive Panorama* Vol 2 (Ian Allan 1966).

Lightweight Baker valve gear operated the 14in diameter piston valves which were set with 1⁹⁄₁₆in lap, ⁵⁄₁₆in lead, and ³⁄₁₆in exhaust clearance. Maximum valve travel was 8½in at 83% cut-off.

Having an engine wheelbase 8ft 1in longer than a 4-6-4, it was important that the new 4-8-4 should be accommodated on the NYC's existing 100ft turntables. Although all its modern 4-6-4 and 4-8-2

engines had been delivered new with large tenders running on two six-wheeled trucks, in order to meet this length requirement a rigid framed 4-10-0 'centipede' tender (officially designated PT5) was attached to the 4-8-4. Water troughs were numerous on the NYC's 'Water Level Route' enabling water capacity to be kept down to a moderate 18,000 US gallons, thus providing more room for a record 46 short tons of coal. The possibility of conveying the entire 75 short tons of coal estimated to be mechanically fired and consumed on an average 928-mile Harmon-Chicago through run had actually been considered, but rejected in favour of a single coaling stop en route at Wayneport, NY.

As an interesting comparison, consider that an LMS 'Duchess' 4-6-2 with 50sq ft of (hand fired) grate could run the 401 miles from Euston to Glasgow on 10 long tons of coal, which suggests that the NYC engines operated at firing rates approaching double that of their British counterparts.

Thoroughly conventional in every respect, the new 4-8-4 represented the ultimate in American steam locomotive technology — or almost the ultimate. To save weight aluminium was employed in the construction of the cab, the running boards and also the smoke deflectors. Although boosters had been applied to all the 4-6-4s they were omitted in the latest 4-8-2s and likewise did not feature either in the 4-8-4.

As delivered, No 6000 had 75in driving wheels and operated at 275lb boiler pressure. However, the boiler was designed to operate at 290lb, the higher pressure to be employed when 79in wheels were fitted — standard with the 4-6-4s. Comparative tests were to determine which diameter was the more suitable.

When brand new No 6000 worked between Harmon and Chicago on some trial trips and then between Harmon and Cleveland for several weeks. In early July 1945 the larger driving wheels were installed

and the prototype began to operate the 'Commodore Vanderbilt' between Harmon and Chicago. Although there was not much in it, with the larger wheels maximum power was developed at a slightly higher speed and so the 79in drivers were retained. During these tests and with its boiler pressed to 290lb, the engine developed a maximum of 6,997ihp at 85mile/h, and 5,375dbhp at 62mile/h. This was the maximum power output ever actually recorded for a two-cylinder locomotive and represented a power to weight ratio exactly twice that achieved by some saturated 4-6-2s built for the NYC in 1907. Indeed, the progressive improvements made in this respect were truly notable as will be seen from the table below:

Class	Wheel Arrangement	Year	Power to weight ratio
Saturated	4-6-2	1907	134lb/ihp
'J1a'	4-6-4	1927	88lb/ihp
'J3a'	4-6-4	1938	76lb/ihp
'S1a'	4-8-4	1945	67lb/ihp

In October 1945 No 6000 was temporarily withdrawn from traffic to undergo strenuous static boiler performance tests at NYC's Selkirk test plant. Here it conformed very closely to — and indeed slightly exceeded — theoretical design expectations. Maximum evaporation was about 110,000lb of superheated steam per hour at a corresponding coal rate of 18,000lb: in service normal evaporation would have been around 70,000lb/hr at a coal rate of 10,000lb. Following this ordeal, No 6000 was scheduled to undergo acceleration tests although by this time further modified engines were being delivered.

Even before No 6000 had been completed, the NYC had placed an order in January 1945 for 25 more

Above: At the head of Chicago–New York express, 'S1b' No 6005 was moving at a fine pace when captured by the Photographer. / Cecil J. Allen Collection

Above right: Alco's works photograph of 'S2a' prototype poppet valve gear equipped locomotive No 5500. / Cecil J. Allen Collection

4-8-4s to be modified as thought desirable from test results obtained from the prototype. Deliveries of these (Class 'S1b', No 6000 was NYC Class 'S1a') commenced in October 1945 with No 6001 and were completed in May 1946 with the appearance of No 6025. The 'S1bs' had 79in drivers and 275lb pressure; tube length was increased from 19ft to 20ft and ashpan capacity from 86cu ft to 98cu ft. This last modification necessitated a complete re-design of the trailing four-wheeled truck with four equal-sized wheels of 41in diameter in place of the former 36in wheels in front, and 44in at rear.

Table 1

NYC No	Class	Alco works Nos	Alco order No	Date of Delivery	Unit Cost
6000	'S1a'	71454	S 1949	March 1945	$255,000
6001-25	'S1b'	73779-73803	S 1980	Oct 1945-May 1946	$238,854
5500	'S2a'	74365	S 1983	June 1946	$290,000

Although the possibility of ordering a 4-4-4-4 'Duplex' version of the standard 4-8-4 from the Baldwin Locomotive Works in June 1945 had at one time been considered, an additional 4-8-4 was ordered from Alco to be fitted with Franklin poppet valve gear. This was the sole occupant of NYC Class 'S2a' and was

numbered 5500. It was provided with two inlet valves of $6\frac{1}{2}$in diameter and three exhaust valves of 6in diameter at each end of either cylinder.

While Nos 6001-25 were in course of delivery, Alco brought into operation a special stress relieving furnace for the production of all-welded locomotive boilers of any size. This development came just too late to apply welded boilers to the 'S1b' engines from new, but one such was fitted to No 5500 built to a separate, later order. Despite a probable saving in weight on this account of the order of 4,000-5,000lb, this engine still weighed 8,000lb more than a standard 'S1b'. In addition, its tender was modified to increase the coal capacity to 47 short tons and to reduce the water capacity to 16,000 US gallons; as a result No 5500's tender weighed 13,300lb less than those behind Nos 6000-25.

Tests to evaluate the merit, or otherwise, of the Franklin valve gear on No 5500 did not take place until June-November 1947 by which time any results obtained were largely academic. They were so arranged as to be directly comparable with results obtained from piston valve No 6023 during the same period the previous year. At speeds above 30mile/h piston valves appeared to yield a marginally higher indicated and drawbar horsepower. This held for normal operating speeds up to about 75mile/h when poppet valves began to show a slight advantage. But No 5500 was notably inferior in acceleration to No 6023. With 15 cars weighing 1,005 short tons gross the latter took 5.02min to accelerate from rest to 75mile/h over a distance of 19,400ft. No 5500, with a comparable load of 1,000 short tons, took 5.20min and 21,000ft. The heavier the loading, the more marked became the discrepancy. Tests with up to 27 cars weighing about 1,900 short tons were made, with No 6023 taking 9.0min and No 5500 no less than 10.5min to reach 75mile/h.

Working at a constant output of 4,000ihp excluding auxiliaries, steam consumption per ihp hour was in favour of No 5500 at 15.4lb compared to 15.8lb and coal, 1.92lb compared to 2.10lb for No 6023. This represented only a relatively minor improvement in thermodynamic efficiency which was markedly outweighed by the much greater maintenance involved and the inferior acceleration characteristics.

Prior to these tests, and soon after delivery, No 5500 participated in some far more important trials. Except for such instances as the New York City-Harmon electrification at the end of World War II, the New York Central was still essentially an all-steam line. However, the diesel-electric locomotive was rapidly advancing, offering certain operating economies that could not be ignored. Realising that it had absolutely first-class steam power in the Niagaras, the NYC decided to make a straight comparison which took place over a six-month period between October 1946 and March 1947.

Six 4,000hp twin-unit diesels experimentally purchased in 1946 were pitted against six 4-8-4s, Nos 6007/9/12/24/5, and poppet valve fitted No 5500. The Niagaras soon showed that they could average 24,000 miles a month, but to achieve this, engine house procedures had to be very highly organised (in their favour) with plenty of major spares, eg wheels on hand. Quarterly inspections kept the engines out of traffic for only 36-48hr, and monthly boiler washouts a mere 8hr. Daily servicing and turning were pared to $2\frac{1}{2}$hr.

It was a closely fought contest as will be seen from Table 2. The diesel only won marginally, but against the inherently low first cost of a modern steam unit, as compared to a diesel, should also be set its equally inherently low drawbar thermal efficiency, about 6% as compared to 22%. This was the most intensive exploitation of steam power ever made, admittedly assisted by the long through runs possible on the NYC, rarely encountered on many other railways on either side of the Atlantic. From delivery in May 1946 until March 1947, with preferential treatment No 6024 ran 227,000 miles during the 11-month period, or effectively 250,000 miles a year!

These tests also showed that, despite slightly greater acceleration over the 0-60mile/h speed range, the diesel took more than half as long and far again to attain 100mile/h when hauling a 15-car train of 1,005

Table 2
NYC Steam v. Diesel-Electric Trials, 1946

	Steam 4-8-4 6,000hp	Diesel-Electric Twin Unit 4,000hp
Unit cost index	100	147
Index cost per hp	100	221
Total annual cost per mile	$1.22	$1.11
Drawbar thermal efficiency	6%	22%

	Passenger	Freight	Passenger	Freight
Annual mileage	288,000	102,000	324,000	120,000
Average monthly mileage	24,000	8,500	27,000	10,000
Utilisation, % (total annual hours)	63.0	63.5	70.4	70.1
Availability, % (total annual hours)	69.0	65.7	74.2	73.5

short tons on level track. The steam 4-8-4 accomplished this in 16.5min over a distance 21.3 miles from rest, while a *triple* unit 6,000hp diesel took precisely 10min longer and required 37.8 miles!

When new, the Niagaras hauled the 'Twentieth Century Limited' to a 16hr New York-Chicago schedule (taking over from electric traction at Harmon, of course) the time being clipped by 30min as from 1 April 1947. This meant hauling 1,000 short tons at an average of 61.7mile/h with 10 intermediate stops. A graphic account by the late W. A. Tuplin of everyday 4-8-4 driving techniques on the NYC appeared in *Trains Illustrated* for April 1952 where he described riding in the cab of No 6025 between Rochester and Albany in 1949.

Before the engines were barely two years old severe cracking of the riveted carbon-silicon steel boiler plates was discovered and commencing in November 1947 and continuing into 1948 24 engines received all-welded boilers from Alco. Allowing for the fact that No 5500 was so equipped from new this left two engines untreated. Three further welded boilers were therefore obtained from the Combustion Engineering Co of Chattanooga, Tennessee, in 1950, Alco having relinquished all its steam locomotive interests early the previous year.

So renewed the NYC 4-8-4s could reasonably have expected to operate well into the 1960s, but such was not to be. Rapid replacement of steam by diesel-electric traction had been decreed as a result of the

1946 trials, and after 1948 diesels were increasingly employed between Harmon and Chicago. Niagaras continued to work out of Harmon, mainly on fast freights, until the summer of 1953, after which they were confined to west of Buffalo. During their last three years of service these majestic machines worked over the Big Four lines to Cincinnati and St Louis. Retirement began early in 1955 when they were barely 10 years old, and the last active survivor is believed to have been No 6015 observed in steam at Indianapolis in late June 1956. Many were consumed in the steel mills of Granite City, Illinois. A number of the 4-8-4s were latterly running with Lima-built 'centipede' tenders originally supplied c1946 for service with Hudsons.

With its roller bearings, welded boiler and poppet valves, No 5500 was arguably the most advanced of all American 4-8-4s, but was also probably the shortest lived. It was retired in 1951 on account of the excessive maintenance costs associated with its poppet valve gear, a downfall shared with the 52 Pennsylvania 'T1' 4-4-4-4s. The actuating mechanism, similar to Walschaerts valve gear, was inaccessibly enclosed between the frames, but in 1947 the manufacturers produced an improved version, designated Type B, which employed instead an external propeller shaft. This received a handful of applications but as a development it came too late to hold back the onrush of dieselisation in North America.

This type of valve gear was to have featured on a projected Lima 4-8-6 outlined in 1949, of which the most notable feature would have been the so-called Lima Double-Belpaire firebox. This was devised at Lima immediately after World War II in order to maximise free gas area which had become the ultimate limiting factor as regards maximum steam production.

Right: The NYC's 'Missourian' passing Peekskill on the last stage of the run from St Louis to Harmon headed by No 6018. An electric locomotive will take over at Harmon for the last 33 miles to New York. / *Cecil J. Allen Collection*

Below: This shot of No 6021 demonstrates the impressiveness of the 'Niagaras'' 115ft length. / *Cecil J. Allen Collection*

Table 3

	4-6-4	4-8-2	4-8-4	4-8-4	4-8-4	4-8-6 (Projected)
Wheel arrangement						
Class	'J3a'	'L4b'	'S1a'	'S1b'	'S2a'	Lima
Built	1937/8	1942/3	1945	1945/6	1946	(1949)
Cylinders (2) (in)	$22\frac{1}{2}\times29$	26×30	25×32	$25\frac{1}{2}\times32$	$25\frac{1}{2}\times32$	28×32
Driving wheels (in)	79	72	75*	79	79	70
Boiler pressure (lb)	275	250	275*	275	275	280
Evaporative heating surface (sq ft)	4,187	4,676	4,632	4,827	4,827	5,263
Superheater (sq ft)	1,745	2,103	1,977	2,060	2,060	2,028
Grate area (sq ft)	82.0	75.3	101.0	101.0	101.0	132.9
Adhesion weight (lb)	195,000	266,500	275,000	275,000	275,000	280,000
Engine weight (lb)	360,000	401,100	471,000	477,000	485,000	525,000
Tender water capacity (US gal)	14,000	15,200	18,000	18,000	16,000	22,000
Coal (short tons)	30	42	46	46	47	26
Overall length (ft in)	95 11	N/A	115 $5\frac{9}{16}$	115 $5\frac{9}{16}$	115 $5\frac{9}{16}$	N/A
Tractive effort (lb)	43,440†	59,900	62,330	61,570	61,570	74,600‡

* 79in/290lb, TE=62,400lb
† booster 12,100lb extra
‡ booster 12,400lb extra

1 short ton=2,000lb=0.893 long tons
1 US Gallon=0.833 imperial gallons

Outside the Pennsylvania RR, the Belpaire firebox was rarely encountered in modern US practice, and in this development of it the combustion chamber was to be of roughly rectangular section. However, this required the lower outside 'shoulders' to be set above the coupled wheels. Lima had envisaged building a demonstration 4-8-6 in 1950, just as it had produced the prototype 2-8-4 in 1925 with such revolutionary results. In maximum height and total wheelbase the proposed 4-8-6 was noticeably aimed at the NYC, whose loading gauge restrictions thereby limited its coupled wheel diameter to 70in. This same nominal dimension, however, had not precluded a Norfolk & Western 4-8-4 from attaining an alleged 110mile/h on the level. At 12.4sq ft the total free gas area in the 4-8-6 would still have worked out at only 9.33% of the grate area, which at 133sq ft would have exceeded that of the majority of Mallet articulateds and equalled that of the immense 2-6-6-6s built by Lima for the Chesapeake & Ohio and Virginian roads.

Although not strictly relevant to the all too brief history of the New York Central 4-8-4s, the stillborn Lima 4-8-6 is of great interest in that it indicated what considerable further development was still possible with the high-speed eight-coupled dual-purpose steam locomotive in North America. Considered in relation to the Niagara such a design should have been capable of somewhere between 8,250 and 9,250ihp, with about 6,500hp available at the drawbar.

The writer is indebted to Messrs Charles M. Smith and P. E. Percy for invaluable assistance in the preparation of this study.

Below: Diagram of Lima's projected 4-8-6 of 1949.

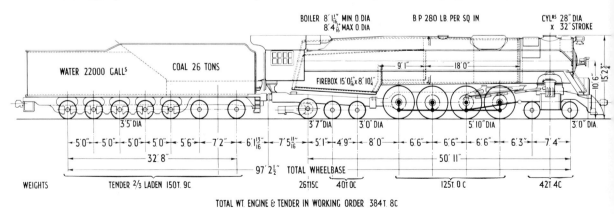

British industrial steam survivors

Even into the late 1970s — over ten years after British Rail dispensed with steam — isolated pockets of steam operation could be found in England, Scotland and Wales. Gradually those locations with regular steam working have gone over to diesel or the mines and plants have shut up shop. NCB No 8 (Robert Stephensons & Hawthorns 7139 of 1944) pauses on the bridge over the River Cynon at Mountain Ash Colliery on 6 April 1978.
/ Michael Rhodes

Above: Littleton Colliery, near Penkridge, Staffs, saw the last steam duty by No 7 (Hudswell Clarke No 1752 of 1944) on 18 February 1977. The locomotive went on to Bickershaw Colliery in Lancashire. / *John Titlow*
Below: A number of collieries and power stations have clung on to industrial steam power as a standby for the regular diesel locomotive. A Robert Stephensons & Hawthorns 16in×12in 0-6-0ST (7412 of 1948) was steamed in the autumn of 1977 at the National Smokeless Fuels Ltd Norwood Coke Works, Newcastle. / *Graeme Binns*

Above right: Bickershaw Colliery, near Wigan, retained steam right to the end of the 1970s. On 13 February 1978 *Warrior*, an 0-6-0ST (Hunslet No 3823 of 1954) and *Bickershaw*, an 0-6-0ST, produce a spectacular effect at the colliery. / *J. D. Nicholls*

Below right: Craig Merthyr Colliery, Pontardulais, near Llanelly, said farewell to steam in 1978. A Bagnall 'Austerity' 0-6-0ST (No 2758 of 1944) shunts at the colliery on 26 May 1978. / *Bob Avery*

Below: Another shot of the Pontardulais system. Bagnall No 2758, again, climbs towards the colliery at Craig Merthyr with empties from Pontardulais on 26 May 1978. / Bob Avery

Above: North of the Border some steam was still at work in 1978. This is NCB's Scottish Area No 9, a Hudswell Clarke 0-6-0T No 895 of 1909, seen pulling strongly in September 1977 when taking coal to Bedlay colliery exchange sidings. / A. Pearson

Learning the road

C. D. WRIGHT

For a BR driver, one of the few fortunate aspects of becoming redundant is that under the well-oiled redundancy and resettlement arrangements there is the opportunity of making two moves in the grade. The system also offers the chance of a move to another depot which otherwise would not be granted, in view of the extensive training involved.

After two pleasant years working at Tilbury, I was notified that my option, placed when I became redundant at Canning Town, had come through and I would be transferred to Cambridge Street depot LMR (formerly Kentish Town shed) the following week.

The railway out of St Pancras appealed to me as did the motive power. The Class 45 is a distinctive machine typical of the early rakish BR diesel designs, which when hauling vacuum fitted stock under semaphore signals, represented a railroading experience that has declined in recent years. I wanted the thrill and sense of prestige associated with express train driving, to me still the railway's premier work. I admit I went for an ideal which to many railwaymen has long since lost its validity and for a glory that had really vanished years before. Since the demise of steam, my interest in railways has turned to the grandeur of the scenery (industrial or country) through which the lines pass and the history, architecture, and civil engineering achievements — which the former Midland system has in plenty.

I took to the Class 45s with immediate enthusiasm. This, of course, is their correct title being adopted officially in place of the former 'Peak' and Type 4 designations. But unofficially, the older names have been less easy to discard and drivers persist in calling them 'fours', and the Class 47s 'four and a half's'.

Grubby in old age they may now be, but it is difficult to find anyone who has a bad word for a '45'. Although affinities obviously exist, they are generally considered to be more powerful than both the Class 46s and 47s. The reason is that the Crompton Parkinson traction equipment seems to draw far more from the Sulzer engine than the Brush equipment of the other two. On semi-fasts, particularly, the Class 45s are consistently superior, notably over the three big banks on the Midland main line — Sharnbrook, Desborough and Kibworth.

It was hard to believe I had known them for 17

Below: Journey's start. 'Not like a monument to the past but to an age which has not arrived' — St Pancras vies with the gasholders in this view as 45.147 leaves with a Nottingham train in March 1975. / Brian Morrison

Above: Splendid sentinel — but this ex-Midland gantry has lost some of its functions with the erosion of freight traffic at Brent. 45.125 dips down to the North Circular Road bridge with a down Sunday Nottingham train. / L. A. Nixon

Left: Doomed by the resignalling associated with the 1982 St Pancras/Moorgate-Bedford electrification is Napsbury's fine show of repeater signals. / P. Butler

years and yet there they were in the face of advanced railway technology still working top link trains. As a 12-year old schoolboy when diesels were unfamiliar in shape and sound I had watched them pass through Kentish Town station. They had all the massiveness and modernity then expected of the new diesel locomotives. You could feel the ground shake beneath your feet as they burst out of the tunnels and passed you by; the noise of the train and the reverberation of the engine merged into a sustained roar. Above all,

pal station for Anglo-Scottish and Manchester traffic. Other economies have meant the loss of duties on Sheffield trains for Cambridge Street crews and of work on some of Leicester semi-fasts withdrawn altogether. In line with my experience at previous depots this loss of work was depressingly familiar.

My initial task was to learn St Pancras and the complexity of metals between there and Silkstream Junction (Hendon). At this stage of my training the sequence of movements and the necessary amount of shunts dictated by the insidious, subsidary signals seemed too great ever to master completely and an impassable stumbling block in learning the road further afield. In contrast to the uniformity of colour light signals which I had been used to previously, the signals and rails seemed strewn in inextricable confusion. Thankfully, I found the Midland drivers, like their LTSR colleagues, friendly and easy with their knowledge. The old regional barriers, it would seem, have been swept away for good except in the memories of the older drivers. As recently as 10-15 years ago, however, it would have been otherwise.

Modernisation has also swept away, not before time, many of the old prejudices although they have not yet been entirely obliterated. The principle of hating your neighbouring depot is common on the railway but this is nothing compared with the ASLEF versus NUR discord. The footplate men have always been a grade apart, separated from their fellows by inclination and origin. In industry generally, pride and closing ranks against outsiders have always knitted tradesmen into tight ranks. On the railway, behind this attitude lay the camaraderie of the footplate with its memories of the past with the misery of early starts, lost weekends of long hours and bad mates. But, on the good side, were the unforgettable thrills, the characters and the halycon days.

After learning the London area I decided the best way to learn the route to the East Midlands was in three sections — the reverse in fact of the Midland's gradual extensions towards London. First, there was the four-track, well-engineered London extension out to Bedford, then the twisting, turning, heavily graded line, evidence of imposed economics, on to Leicester. Finally, the oldest, but most altered, Midland Counties' section forward to Nottingham and Derby. Unlike its former partner in the LMSR, down the road at Euston, so rebuilt in recent years that it is practically a new railway, the Midland's face remains unchanged in almost all except motive power. Distinctive Midland architecture defines its frontiers clearly, the southern end guarded by the magnificient and unique St Pancras standing not like a monument to the past but to an age which has not yet arrived.

Nottingham and Leicester stations loom above the traffic-choked streets making a startling contrast with the stark utility of the modern buildings going up all

there was the noise of the turbochargers going full blast. Sounding like a banshee wail, they put out a ferocious sound intensified by echoes from the high surrounding walls: 'Rumbling under blackened girders, Midland, bound for Cricklewood,' as John Betjeman has so evocatively put in words an earlier Midland age.

From April to August I was given the task of learning the route to Trent and the Derby and Nottingham branches. This is as far as Cambridge Street crews now work.

Many complain that with the end of hot and dirty work on the steam engine most of the glamour of the job has been lost. Meanwhile, in parallel, Kings Cross has become the main terminal for Leeds and Bradford and since electrification Euston has become the princi-

Left: Replaced by the new Bedford station in the autumn of 1978, the shadows are heavy at Bedford Midland Road in April 1977. / I. P. Cowley

Below left: 45.102 hammers past the still important Wellinborough yards with the 14.50 Nottingham-St Pancras on 4 March 1976. / Philip D. Hawkins

Right: A 'four and a half', then still numbered 1566, roars up the 1 in 176 gradient out of Elstree Tunnel with the 16.50 St Pancras-Nottingham on 16 June 1973. / Brian Morrison

Below: A signal check has caused this Class 45 to produce smoke and not the gradient for its parcels train is now descending the 1 in 119 of the bank past Sharnbrook box on 13 July 1973. / John E. Oxley

around them. Derby is the poorest of the three big East Midland stations, having suffered from war damage and postwar mass concrete rebuilding. But, Wellingborough, Kettering and Loughborough with their glass ridge and furrow canopies and ornate iron column supports still serve to characterise the old Company.

Towards the end of my road learning, and not many weeks before starting diesel training, I rode a late night express from Derby to London with driver Jim McArthur, during a week when the Midlands and Southern England suffered their worst rain for years.

The rain had been falling in solid sheets for hours, rivers had overflowed their banks, roads were flooded, and in some areas trains had been diverted or cancelled. With the wheels pounding the track and the familiar whine from the engine at our backs, we hurtled through the night, the rain harried by a strong wind blasted against the squat nose of our locomotive, *The Royal Marines*. The countryside about was black and ill-defined: even the road bridges we raced under merged with the darkness and remained hidden until the last moment. As my mind tried to picture the road ahead, I began secretly to doubt my own judgement. On such nights once familiar shapes and views can become fearfully unfamiliar. Away from towns, apart from the sparkle of lights from occasional far-off farmhouses, the faint signal lights are the only sure guide to your locality. I gazed across to the silent figure of Jim sitting slightly hunched forward in his seat as he searched intently for the pinpoint of light ahead that would tell if Glendon's semaphore distant was at clear or caution. Like so many of his breed he showed complete confidence on that, the blackest of nights.

Finally, at the very end of my training, I allowed my interest to wander beyond my road learning timetable. The Midland had rivals in the East Midlands, lines that are no longer a threat. Their remains provided me with a nostalgic interlude. The formidable Great Central, which paralleled the Midland to London, still provides physical remains. Tunnels, bridges and embankments can be seen at various locations en route and not far from the Midland stations the GC's viaducts can be seen boldly crossing the city streets of Leicester and Nottingham.

The Ambergate, Nottingham and Boston and Eastern Junction Railway was a company formed to link Derbyshire with the east coast. Grantham to Nottingham was as far as they reached before being taken over by the Great Northern. This brought the foreigner not only to Nottingham but, after further extensions, into the heart of the Midland at Derby. Nottingham Low Level and Derby Friargate, the Great Northern's two principal stations, were still intact at the time of my travels, although the latter was derelict and due for demolition.

The powerful LNWR's influence in Midland territory was restricted to a few cross-country lines linking the Nor'West with the GN. Most are now closed, their twisting trackbeds and earthworks leaving scars across the picturesque Northamptonshire and Leicestershire countryside. The most substantial monument remaining to the intervention of the LNWR is the station at Market Harborough looking as different from the standard Midland architecture on the Leicester-Hitchin extension as it is possible to do so, and now successfully renovated.

The expansive Midland has also suffered contraction. I followed the trackbed of the pioneer Leicester and Swannington Railway from Leicester West Bridge (a garage now stands on the site of the station) along a well-defined path to Glenfield Tunnel. The much photographed western portal was well hidden in an overgrown cutting off Station Road opposite the Railway Hotel. These names, I hope, at least will survive to remind locals and mystify travellers.

Background railway reading on forgotten railways gave a good introduction to the area but I visited the sites with only a local map to guide me. Facts and figures are unnecessary to absorb the atmosphere and to slide back into the past or, indeed, appreciate the present. Your own emotional reaction makes things come alive. Nevertheless, too much nostalgia can become a solemn business. After such searchings it was always good to return to the cab of my locomotive and enjoy the business of the present railway.

Below: Home of the Midland Railway — Derby. 45.149 winds its Sheffield-St Pancras express out of the station on 22 April 1976 contemplated by a Swindon-built 'Cross-Country' unit. / John E. Oxley

A final trip to Brecon

J. M. TOLSON

Christmas Eve 1962 was a fine sunny day and, as we had for once completed our shopping in good time and did not have to join the frenzied last-minute rush to buy presents, my wife and I decided to visit Brecon before all its passenger services were withdrawn. I had intended to visit Brecon the previous month and indeed went as far as Three Cocks and thence up the Mid-Wales line to Builth Road between the bracken covered slopes of the Upper Wye valley, but, while waiting for the 14.50 Moat Lane Junction-Brecon, I learned that, unbeknown to me, the Neath & Brecon services had been withdrawn some three weeks previously on 15 October and, as this rendered my plans useless, regretfully retraced my steps to Hereford.

For our December trip we decided to approach Brecon over the former Brecon & Merthyr line from Newport which would provide us with an exciting and picturesque journey of almost $2\frac{1}{2}$ hours through varied scenery. A good journey on the 09.43 from Gloucester found us in Newport just after 10.30 which gave us plenty of time to purchase our tickets and get something to eat before boarding the 11.15 to Brecon. Our train consisted of '57xx' 0-6-0PT No 4679 and two corridor coaches; it was clear, too, that we were not the only enthusiasts making the journey.

In due course No 4679, exuding great clouds of steam, slowly moved its train past the station sidings with the civic buildings dominating the hill to the right, and plunged into Hillfield Tunnel. After emerging into bright sunlight again, our train left the main line to Cardiff and West Wales at Gaer Junction and climbed northwards through the short Gaer Tunnel. As we gained the higher ground, we were able to look back over the docks and see the lines of the former Alexandra Docks & Railway Company which were to join us at Park Junction. Here we found overselves on one of six parallel tracks, two of which had belonged to the AD&R and the remaining four to the GWR. This section of track was known as the Tredegar Park Golden Mile because of the enormous tolls collected by the landowner through whose land it ran. We descended towards Bassaleg and crossed the River Ebbw as our train parted company with the GWR Western Valley lines to Aberbeeg, Brynmawr and Ebbw Vale, which lost their passenger services as from 30 April 1962.

We were now travelling over the metals of the former Brecon & Merthyr Railway and it was at Bassaleg (three miles) that this company's largest freight yard and engine shed were to be found; even in 1962 it remained a busy centre for mineral traffic. Just before the station we passed the trailing junction which marked the end of the AD&R line.

The B&M station at Bassaleg was of wooden construction with its main buildings and signalbox on the left and a small shelter on the right. Our train did not waste any time here but moved off through a maze of sidings filled with wagons, leaving the River Ebbw to follow the Western Valley lines as we headed northwards on a shelf cut into the hillside overlooking gloomy factories and a large power station. Climbing at 1 in 82 we struggled manfully past Rhiwderin ($4\frac{1}{4}$ miles), closed in 1952, a small stone building on the up side, and still climbing found ourselves entering the higher reaches of the valley with bracken covered hills closing in on the line and isolated farm houses perched on the hillside. The line zig-zagged over a series of sharp curves and it was here that we passed two old B&M somersault signals and also another closed station at Church Road ($6\frac{1}{4}$ miles). Here the stone buildings on the left and small shelter on the right echoed the somewhat desolate nature of this spot with their broken windows, a feeling which was heightened by a quarry whose chute crossed over the line as it began to level out after the somewhat sinuous climb through what in summer must be a very pleasant part of rural Monmouthshire.

Between Rhiwderin and Machen the mountains began to close in and we entered the southern end of the Rhymney Valley and from here caught a first glimpse of the collieries in the distance. The River Rhymney marks the border between Monmouthshire and Glamorganshire and our first impression that the western side of the valley was more industrialised was borne out as we travelled farther to the north. As we approached Machen ($7\frac{1}{4}$ miles), set half in the valley and half on the celebrated Machen Mountain, we saw traces of the B&M locomotive department headquarters and repair shops. The main station buildings here consisted of a long canopy between two stone buildings on the down side and a stone goods shed. The track had been a prize length in 1958 but our

attention was distracted by the arrival of 0-6-0PT No 4627 heading the 10.52 from New Tredegar.

Machen was also the junction for the short branch to the Rhymney Railway at Caerphilly which was authorised in 1861 and opened in 1864. The branch was of interest in that it consisted of two separate single lines, the first of which had a falling gradient towards Caerphilly of 1 in 39. The second, or Machen loop line, was constructed at a grade of 1 in 200 and opened on 14 September 1891. This was built to allow the passage of eastbound through coal trains from Pontypridd to Newport and formed a section of a route in which the metals of no less than five separate pre-Grouping companies were traversed in 18 miles. The B&M, although the owning company, concerned itself solely with mineral traffic and never worked passenger services which were handled after their inception in 1887 by the AD&R, GWR and Rhymney Railway. The Pontypridd-Machen passenger services were withdrawn on 15 September 1956.

Moving away from Machen over the sharply curving line, we were able to look westwards across the valley towards Caerphilly and its imposing castle over which hung a thick pall of smoke from industrial Glamorganshire. But we were soon to enter an isolated patch of industry on the Monmouthshire side of the Rhymney Valley. At Trethomas ($9\frac{1}{2}$ miles), a small corrugated iron station on the up side (opened in 1915), we saw our first large colliery with two '56xx' 0-6-2Ts shunting in the neighbourhood.

Bedwas ($10\frac{3}{4}$ miles) was of interest because the main station buildings still had a board bearing the title 'GWR Special Notices', but our driver was impatient to continue his arduous journey. We curved away northwards into the countryside while in the valley could be seen miners' houses and the benzol and tar distillery with its waste heaps and storage tanks. We caught sight of the remains of the former Barry Railway's Llanbradach viaduct which had spanned the valley to join the B&M at Duffryn Isaf. This was opened on 2 January 1905 for mineral traffic only, but was little used after the Grouping and demolished in 1937. In the meantime, we were unaware of the Rhymney Railway's line from Cardiff to Rhymney

and Nantybwch which ran on the other side of the
valley at a somewhat lower level, and which remained
parallel with our route for some distance. Although
many of the narrow Welsh valleys are filled with
polluted rivers and depressing collieries, slagheaps and
miners' houses, even in the worst places it is possible
to climb swiftly out of the valleys on to the relatively
unspoiled hillsides. In the Rhymney Valley, in
particular, there is little of this depressing industrial
waste and the high level of the B&M line enabled the
traveller to make the most of the view and the pleasant
hillsides.

Soon, however, we approached the town of
Hengoed, spread on the far slope of the valley and in
the valley itself. The B&M station was known as
Maesycwmmer (15¼ miles) and the line was crossed
shortly afterwards by the high viaduct carrying the
GWR's cross-country line from Pontypool Road to
Neath. Over on the far side of the valley the high level
(GWR) station at Hengoed could be seen with
immediately below the Rhymney's station. At
Maesycwmmer Junction we passed the connecting
spur (opened on 28 December 1863) from the high
level GWR line and soon reached the delightfully
named station of Fleur-de-lis Platform (16½ miles),
known locally as 'The Flower'. The booking office
here was set back off the platform at right angles to
the track, and the dilapidated GWR seats gave the
whole station a desolate appearance.

From here the 11.15 from Newport continued to
climb in a shallow cutting past a colliery to Pengam
(17¼ miles). This stone-built station was known more
specifically as Pengam (Mon) to distinguish it from
Pengam (Glam), the Rhymney's station in another
county, although only separated from the B&M by a
narrow valley. Leaving Pengam, we climbed past
another colliery and in due course swept over to join
the RR line at Aberbargoed Junction, while the B&M
line continued its course northwards to New Tredegar
and Rhymney. Due to earth movements, the section of
line between New Tredegar and Rhymney was closed
on 14 April 1930, the last named being served by
trains from the RR line, and the line was then singled
between New Tredegar and Aberbargoed Junction.
Latterly, there were three trains a day between

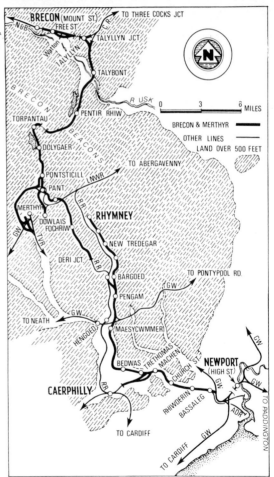

Newport and New Tredegar, but up to six additional (including workmen's) trains covered sections of the line, some having connections with Newport-Brecon services. The Newport-New Tredegar passenger services were withdrawn from 31 December 1962.

After climbing slowly through the somewhat depressing valley piled high with slagheaps and the hillsides dotted with houses and collieries, our train edged past some large cooling towers and arrived at Bargoed having covered $18\frac{3}{4}$ miles in just under an hour. On the face of it, this was extremely slow going but for almost the whole distance the gradient had been against us — and worse was to come.

At Bargoed the engine paused for a well-earned drink enabling a look round the station, the largest so far seen on our journey (and with three platform faces), being served also by the trains from Cardiff to Rhymney, and originally the property of the Rhymney Railway.

Returning to the train it was to discover that as the water supply had frozen up, No 4679 had still not been able to replenish its tanks. Crew and station staff were forced to climb to the top of the water tower at the north end of the island platform and finally managed to get the pipes clear, and some 20min late we set out in a determined effort to make up for lost time.

Almost immediately the RR line to Rhymney curved away north-eastwards over a viaduct and we climbed along a rocky shelf on the side of the hill with the road and the River Bargoed Rhymney in the valley below. Although continuing to climb, now on the western side of the valley, the valley floor rose more quickly and, after passing a colliery with platforms for

miners' trains, we ran through bracken covered hills and found ourselves almost at the bottom of a high level valley to reach Darran & Deri (21 miles), furnished with a corrugated iron structure on the up side and a wooden building on the right. The $2\frac{1}{4}$-mile section of Rhymney Railway metals from Aberbargoed Junction terminated in an end-on junction with the Brecon & Merthyr just south of Ogilvie Village Halt ($21\frac{1}{2}$ miles) which was a corrugated iron shelter on a short platform on the up side. The track became single here and the gradient stiffened to 1 in 40. In common with the rest of the B&M single track sections (except the section of the Merthyr branch between Morlais Junction and Rhydycar Junction where the electric train staff was used), this section was worked by electric train token. The other track did not end immediately, but continued at a lower level along the valley floor, terminating in sidings. After passing a colliery halt and the accompanying slagheaps, and now surrounded by increasingly desolate and bare hillsides, we arrived at the old, but dying mining village of Fochriw ($23\frac{3}{4}$ miles), the station having a passing loop and staggered platforms. The gradient had now slackened to 1 in 300, but our train then curved almost at right angles into a vicious 1 in 38 for half a mile and No 4679 was forced to give of her best. The scenery gradually grew more and more desolate culminating in open moorland dotted with sheep and wild-looking ponies and pitted with small canyons. Hereabouts, 25 miles from Newport, the 11.15 reached the summit of the line (1,314ft above sea level) at Pantywaun, having made a continuous climb from sea level.

The desolate nature of the moor gave some idea of

the dreadful winter snowdrifts experienced earlier in 1962 (and previously), while an open cast mine was a reminder that formerly the whole region was covered with coal and iron workings and criss-crossed with a maze of small railway lines. The country surrounding Pantywaun Halt (25¾ miles), a small platform with a derelict and closed office at a lower level, is perhaps the most desolate spot I have ever seen. Scarred ground, evil looking pools and the ruined houses of a small, almost deserted village conjured up such a feeling of decay and depression that it was good to be on the move again, this time to descend for almost five miles at a ruling gradient of up to 1 in 50.

Just north of Pantywaun, we passed over the course of the former LNWR line from Merthyr to Tredegar and Abergavenny and, skirting the town of Dowlais, arrived at Dowlais Top (26½ miles). There had been a surprisingly large influx of passengers at Fochriw, and now there was an equal exodus. At first sight amazing, since Dowlais Top was as desolate as Pantywaun, it was revealed that this was the best place to catch a bus into Dowlais and Merthyr.

Having disgorged the crowd, the train set off past the connection with the LNWR Abergavenny line (lifted about 1933), giving a fine view over the valley with the Taf Fechan reservoirs in the distance as it curved away over a stream towards Pant (28¼ miles) where the short branch from Dowlais joined the Brecon line.

Near the station were some ventilating shafts belonging to a tunnel on the abandoned LNWR line from Abergavenny which reached Merthyr by a very circuitous course and passed under the Brecon & Merthyr line no less than four times in 1½ miles. The Brecon & Merthyr had obtained powers for the 1¼-mile single line branch from Pant to a terminus near the iron works at Dowlais in 1865 and it was opened on 23 June 1869. Like most Brecon & Merthyr lines the gradients were formidable with a falling gradient of 1 in 40 towards Dowlais. Scheduled to a one-minute stop at Pant, in view of our lateness we paused only for seconds and then descended to the valley of the Taf Fechan and entered the former county of Brecknock. Approaching Pontsticill Junction (29¾ miles) — opened in 1867 — the branch from Merthyr came in on the left from the wooded ravine and its junction with the LNWR Abergavenny line to join the main line just south of the station. The opening of this line in 1868 removed the legal obstructions from inaugurating a through service between Brecon and Newport, delayed until the opening of the Merthyr branch, although the Brecon & Merthyr extension through Dowlais Top to Deri and the end-on junction with the Rhymney Railway had been completed in 1865, and the RR line from Bargoed to Deri had been ready for use the year

Above left: The 11.15 Newport-Brecon of 2 May 1959 is waiting to proceed north from Torpantau now that 0-6-0PT No 3662 has arrived with the 12.15 from Brecon.

Above: A bus is standing outside Dowlais Top station on 14 August 1957 as '57xx' 0-6-0PT No 3634 restarts the 12.15 Brecon-Newport. / Both: S. Rickard

Below: Free Street station at Brecon, '2251' 0-6-0 No 2227 is ready to leave with a Newport train in the early 1950s. / L. King

previously. A service of three trains a day between Brecon and Newport was inaugurated on 1 September 1868, and ran into the Dock Street station at Newport, being transferred to the new High Street station in 1880.

The Merthyr branch itself was a great feat of engineering, as the 6¾ miles from Pontsticill Junction involved a continuous descent of 1 in 45 to 1 in 50 and two massive stone viaducts of 455ft and 770ft respectively were required to carry the line first over the Taf Fechan, and then over the Taf Fawr. Despite the formidable gradients and the viaducts, the track still had to double back upon itself before reaching Merthyr. The section between Morlais Junction and Merthyr became jointly owned with the LNWR in 1875 and services began from the LNWR Tredegar line via a new connection on 1 June 1879. The much reduced ordinary passenger service of two trains each way on weekdays only was withdrawn from the branch from 13 November 1961.

Just before reaching Pontsticill Junction, the 12.10 from Brecon passed being hauled by the inevitable '57xx' 0-6-0PT — No 9679 — and here we were still some 15min down. The station was more imposing than most of the stations on the line, possessing three platform faces with a small but quite elaborately canopied shelter on the island platform. With but a momentary pause, the '57xx' climbed alongside the delightful Taf Fechan Reservoir almost as far as Dolygaer (31½ miles) — the only station without a passing loop between Fochriw and Talyllyn. To the north towered the Brecon Beacons as the Pannier tank toiled up the three-mile ascent mostly at 1 in 47, 52 and 55. Here things became a little hectic as there were quite a few photographers on the train and only one or two open windows. After a somewhat painful climb, from which it appeared that No 4679 was racked to the frames, Torpantau (33 miles) was finally achieved and there was a minute's pause at this inspiringly wild and lonely spot. The combined house and station buildings on the right were solidly built with a large water tower while on the left was a small shelter and the signalbox. Now the line turned sharply eastward and entered the 666yd long Beacon or Summit Tunnel which passed beneath the 'col' at the head of the Collwn valley and was 1,313ft above sea level at the west end. After the tunnel the line turned sharply northwards again and descended the celebrated Seven Mile Bank amid the wonderful scenery of Glyn Collwn towards the River Usk at Talybont. The Seven Mile Bank was built on a shelf cut into the hillside and descended for half a mile at 1 in 68 and then the remaining 6½ miles at 1 in 38 so that southbound trains had to climb 925ft in seven miles.

Although Torpantau is only seven miles from Brecon, the rail journey was almost double in length as the line curved north-eastward to Pentir Rhiw (37 miles), an island platform and passing place with little more than a signalbox and no visible signs of life and no approach by road, but affording an unrivalled view over the Talybont Reservoir. Signalling arrangements here were worthy of note. There was a siding rising sharply into the side of the hill, designed to stop runaways, the normal setting of the road being into the siding; only when the signalman heard the engine whistle that all was well did he set the road right through. The signalman, incidentally, issued tickets here through a window in the side of his box.

Another three miles of this wonderful descent with views of the waterfalls across the valley and we had reached Talybont-on-Usk (40¼ miles) at a height of 385ft above sea level. Our train had hurtled downhill on the down grade as though it were never going to stop, despite the overall restriction of 40mile/h. Now on the valley floor the Brecon & Newport Canal was crossed before entering the station with its large stone buildings and passing loop and what seemed to be a derelict engine shed north of the station. Leaving Talybont, and crossing the River Usk, No 4679 had to climb hard again with gradients of 1 in 56 and 1 in 40 as it headed north-west and passed the eastern avoiding line which heralded Talyllyn Junction (43 miles). Here we met Mogul No 46518 with the 13.20 Brecon-Moat Lane Junction. The final station at Talyllyn Junction was opened on 1 October 1869, as previously both the Brecon & Merthyr and Mid-Wales had their own temporary stations here — the remains of the latter could still be seen in 1962 at the eastern end of the triangle. An extension platform was added in 1895 on the northern side of the triangle to allow trains to Three Cocks to draw up if another train from Brecon was close behind. There were rows of sidings within the triangle and up to 1923 there was also a B&M engine shed. The eastern side of the triangle was opened by the B&M in 1864 and was used extensively by through goods traffic and excursions from South Wales to the Cambrian section. Talyllyn was also on the Midland Railway's through freight route from Swansea to London via Hereford, and from 1877 through passenger trains ran between Swansea and Hereford over Neath & Brecon metals and then over the isolated Midland section to Swansea Victoria but this service ended on 1 January 1931. Although freight traffic after the Grouping was much reduced, as the need for so many competitive routes disappeared, the construction of the dam in the Claerwen Valley brought a large traffic in cement between Merthyr and Rhayader on the Mid-Wales line.

Then in the late 1950s, when the Abergavenny-Brynmawr-Dowlais line was closed to freight traffic, the liquid ammonia tanker trains from Dowlais to Haverton Hill in Durham were re-routed to Hereford via Talyllyn and Three Cocks. The empty tankers left Hereford about noon and the return working of loaded wagons arrived back at Talyllyn around 20.30/21.00, the usual motive power being a WR 0-6-0PT assisted by a similar engine for part or all of the journey — depending on the size of the load. But, apart from this through traffic and the occasional troop trains from Sennybridge on the Neath & Brecon line, there were only two freight trains per day in each direction passing through Talyllyn — one to and from Newport and one to and from Moat Lane Junction, as the daily freight from Hereford terminated at Three Cocks Junction.

Leaving Talyllyn, we plunged immediately into the 674yd long tunnel (originally constructed for the Hay Railway in 1816) and hurried past Groesffordd Halt (45 miles) before entering the outskirts of Brecon. Free Street station (47 miles) was soon reached, a large and imposing brick building on the northern platform here originally housing the general offices of the Brecon & Merthyr Railway before their dispersal to various parts of the system. There was also a terminal bay, the remains of a turntable at the eastern end of this platform, an island platform and a signalbox to the south of this. Free Street was also of note in being one of the largest stations in the country with platforms unconnected by either a footbridge or subway.

Its duty completed, we then traced No 4679 to the shed, near to the original Walton station in Brecon. The long two-road shed was empty but two '2251' 0-6-0s and an Ivatt 2-6-0 were standing by the coaling stage. Before long, '57xx' 0-6-0PT No 8702 passed on

the 14.05 to Newport, but a less pleasant side of the trip came when I visited the shedmaster and found him doling out redundancy notices to the staff as the impending almost complete withdrawal of rail facilities from the town removed the need for a motive power depot. The first stage of the withdrawals had already come in October with the withdrawal of the Neath & Brecon passenger services and on 31 December 1962, the remaining passenger services from Newport, Hereford and Moat Lane Junction were withdrawn, leaving a daily freight from the Newport direction as Brecon's only rail contact with the world at large.

Our day trip continued on another of the doomed lines serving Brecon when we boarded the 16.10 to Hereford, headed by '57xx' No 4679 which had already hauled us from Newport. From Hereford we completed our day trip at Worcester, having covered almost 90 miles on railways due to be closed to passengers at one fell swoop.

This, then, is a cameo of a typical enthusiast's outing on the railways of the early 1960s, unchanged for so long but destined to disappear very quickly, so that nearly 20 years later it seems like recalling the scene of another century.

Below: Staple power on the B&M route, '57xx' 0-6-0PTs Nos 9676/4690 appropriately head the last regular double-headed freight from Brecon-Merthyr as it arrives at Talybont on Usk on 30 August 1963. / B. J. Ashworth

North British Type 2 diesels

CHRIS LEIGH

Under BR's Modernisation Plan, the North British Locomotive Company of Glasgow was the only former steam locomotive manufacturer to receive major orders in its own right for diesel locomotives. The company was not a stranger to diesel or electric traction, however, having been mechanical parts' contractor for a number of export orders through the late 1940s and 1950s. While others, such as Hunslet, ventured into the production of modest diesel shunters, and Beyer Peacock later entered the picture with a single class, the 'Hymek', the pilot scheme orders went in the main to Brush, English Electric, AEI and to BR workshops. Except, that is, for the concerted effort of North British to enter the field for BR's main line diesel locomotive fleet with various types from 800hp to 2,000hp. Five classes were produced, three of which employed hydraulic transmission. Four of the five classes had the NBL/MAN quick-running engine, while the fifth comprised a total of only 10 locomotives. All these factors put the locomotives outside BR's locomotive fleet standardisation of the mid-1960s, and consequently all were victims of early withdrawal, particularly as NBL had ceased operations by then. The North British diesels have now passed into history, but in the early days of BR dieselisation they were concentrated at particular depots and thus became a familiar sight in certain localities.

A common mechanical parts design was produced for two designs in the 1,000/1,500hp range, one having electric and the other hydraulic transmission, and these two classes are worthy of further study. The initial order for six diesel-hydraulics of 1,000hp was placed in January 1956 as part of the plan to equip the Western Region with diesel-hydraulic traction. These locomotives were to employ engines and transmissions of the same type as those used in the 2,000hp diesel-hydraulics which were also ordered from NBL. Subsequently the class was increased to a total of 58, the balance having been ordered in 1957, these having slightly uprated engines and design detail differences.

The first of the class, No D6300, appeared in 1959, with the uprated version entering traffic a year later. The power plant was a 12-cylinder engine designed by MAN of Germany and produced under licence by NBL. It was rated at 1,000bhp in the first six locomotives but this was increased to 1,100bhp for the rest of the class. The Voith-North British three-stage torque converter was fitted; with this unit, simultaneous emptying and filling of each stage of the torque converter provided a smooth automatic changeover with no interruption to the drive as each change was made.

The body superstructure made use of a substantial amount of aluminium for framing, sides and cabs, and the styling was a snub-nosed and shortened version of the sister NBL 'Warship' class. Although it was very much a first generation design, it was unique to the

manufacturer representing a refreshing departure from the angular shape which eventually became the norm for British diesels. A communicating tunnel with doors and a flexible gangway was provided at each end of the locomotive for use when running in multiple, although in practice it was seldom used after the earliest days. The windscreens were curved downwards to provide maximum visibility but gave a visually weak front end design. The driver's controls were grouped in a simple panel below the left-hand screen, with the customary vacuum train brake handle and separate locomotive air brake handle. The usual specification of cab heating, windscreen demisting, food locker and hotplate was complied with, as well as controls for foam fire extinguishers fitted to the engine and train heating boiler. Clayton steam heating boilers were fitted to the first 20 locomotives and the remainder carried the Stone type.

All locomotives were delivered in the standard BR green livery with a grey horizontal stripe at frame height, and numbering was from D6300 upwards. Following usual WR practice with new locomotive types, D6300 commenced working from Swindon on the turns usually employed for running-in steam locomotives. The last of the original batch, D6305, was completed in January 1960, and thereafter deliveries were spasmodic. Although D6305 was delivered in August 1959, it was returned to North British, and D6306/7 of the production batch actually preceded it into traffic. Apart from nominally increased power, the production locomotives had a wider range of multiple unit options, and a modified internal layout which enabled several small external grilles to be tidied up into one large panel. Only two of the class, D6335/6, were delivered in 1961 and no further deliveries were made until March 1962. This was reported as enabling NBL to concentrate on production of the D833 series 'Warships', but in reality denoted the company's increasing financial problems.

After a month's trials D6300 was transferred to Plymouth Laira, where it was joined by the new deliveries as they entered service. Only Nos D6336/7 went directly to Newton Abbot and D6355-7 were delivered to Bristol Bath Road in August-November 1962, although both these depots subsequently received others transferred from Laira. The total dieselisation of services in Cornwall and part of Devon was the first stage of the WR scheme, and the Type 2s, as they were classified, were set to work immediately on a wide range of duties. At the outset they were used in pairs for many duties, standing in for 'Warships' which were in short supply, and particularly over the South Devon banks. Pairings were helpful in the event of failure of one of the locomotives, not uncommon with the teething troubles experienced with a new

Below left: This shot of NB diesel-hydraulic No D 6323 clearly shows the propeller shafts driving to the bogies. The locomotive is hauling an up mixed freight near Bedminster, Bristol, on 3 December 1967. / P. J. Fowler

Above: A pristine pair of Type 2 hydraulics (Nos D6301/2) pass Tuffley Junction on a test train from Swindon Works on 15 January 1959. / P. J. Sharpe

design, and indeed, some pairs double-headed with 'Warships' or steam.

In the early days of January 1960 Nos D6308/11 were turned out at Swindon for the 07.50 Taunton-Bristol-Paddington, returning home on an afternoon parcels working. One member of the class carried out some trials on the Looe branch, while D6310 had its train heating boiler removed for instruction purposes at Laira and was relegated to Hemerdon banking duties. From 11 April 1960 there was a daily duty on the Par-Newquay branch, again employing a pair of the locomotives. Indeed, only banking turns and an afternoon return trip from Plymouth to Exeter via Okehampton were performed by single locomotives, the return train being the Plymouth section of the 15.00 ex-Waterloo. Most other workings involved local passenger turns where they replaced steam locomotives while dmus, like the 'Warships', were under construction. On 12 May a Type 2 failed on the 09.10 Plymouth-Penzance and was replaced by a dmu which had been on a crew training run, and which was probably the first dmu to carry passengers into Penzance. By the summer of 1960 reliability had improved although multiple unit working continued and resulted in some unusual triple-headed workings. On 18 June the 07.50 Newquay to Manchester was headed by D800 with D6311/24 assisting, while a month later when D6306 failed on Hayle bank while partnering D6309 the pair was assisted by a pannier tank.

As deliveries of 'Warships' displaced them from the principal passenger services the Type 2s settled into local freight work and those passenger services not handled by dmus. They covered both freight and passenger workings on the Helston branch until closure, and the six original locomotives were often employed working from St Blazey on the local china clay sidings. By the mid-1960s the class had developed their familiar look — often stained white with china clay dust, or else battle scarred with patches of bare metal demonstrating the incompatibilities of paint, aluminium and the Laira washing plant.

When the WR assumed control of the Southern's routes west of Exeter the Type 2s became common motive power on these lines, working to Ilfracombe, Bude and Padstow as well as on the Southern route from Plymouth to Exeter. Those of the class based at Bristol Bath Road were used mainly on local freight work, and from 1964 they were displaced from or assisted on this work by Class 14 0-6-0s. These, the D9500s, the last and shortest-lived of the BR diesel-hydraulics, were 650hp centre-cab locomotives with rigid frame and coupled wheels. Many of them had a service life of only four years before being sold to the National Coal Board and private industries. However, while they were at Bristol they enabled the NBL Type 2s to be transferred to Old Oak Common where they took over from steam the empty stock workings to and from Paddington, and many local freight duties. In 1967, displaced by Class 31s, many of then returned to Bristol following the demise of the Class 14s, and some also went to the Gloucester area.

From 1966 members of the class were repainted in the standard blue livery, the first four to be so treated receiving yellow end panels instead of the full yellow end which was subsequently adopted; even so, 30 of them were withdrawn in green livery. The only other major change in appearance was the fitting of pairs of two-digit headcode displays to all but one of those locomotives originally built without them. By this time the decline in local trip workings, the rationalisation of the diesel fleet under the National Traction Plan and the decision to standardise on electric transmission had combined to bring the demise of the class. Under the latest BR classification system they became Class 22 but none survived to carry the new numbering; by the late 1960s availability had settled down in the area of 85% but utilisation was low.

Withdrawal began with D6301 in December 1967, followed by the other five prototypes and 20 of the main batch in 1968, several having had very short lives, D6347 lasting only five years nine months. A motive power shortage then brought a stay of execution, during which time the survivors were concentrated at Laira until the end of 1971. The very last working of a member of the class would seem to have been a return trip over the Hemyock branch made by D6339 on 1 January 1972. After this, the Class 22s were towed in succession to Bristol St Phillips Marsh Depot from where they were mostly despatched to Swindon or to Cashmores at Newport for cutting up. They would have been an appropriate type for useful preservation on one of the working preserved lines (one coming very close to being privately purchased), but they just failed to survive into the diesel preservation era.

At the same time that the six original Class 22s were ordered, the BTC placed an order for 10 diesel-electrics of similar specification from North British, with GEC as the electrical equipment supplier. This combination of manufacturers was to be expected as GEC and NBL had been partners for a number of export diesel and electric locomotives. Although they were outwardly similar in appearance to the

NB's Type 2s compared: Above left: is diesel hydraulic No D 6343 on a trip working down the Lambourn branch to RAF Welford on 5 April 1969. / *D. E. Canning*

Above: is an official shot of a diesel-electric. Their departure from East Anglia was unmourned; No D 6129 stands on a sugar beet train outside Bury St Edmunds' beet factory in November 1959. / *BR*

hydraulics, they were longer and heavier as a result of the use of electric transmission. Their development paralleled the sister class in many respects, not least of these being that subsequent orders increased the total of locomotives to 58. The first 30 locomotives were intended for Eastern Region use, with the remainder being assigned to the Scottish Region.

Like their WR sisters, the first 10 locomotives were rated at 1,000hp, with subsequent deliveries uprated to 1,100hp, although many of these ran for extended periods downrated. The cab ends and external features were also similar to the WR units, but internally the aluminium body structure was divided into four compartments by transverse bulkheads. These separated the two cabs, engine room and electrical compartments. End gangways were provided for coupling to a second locomotive when working in multiple. Locomotives intended for the Eastern Region were fitted with a stepped control system, while those for the Scottish Region had the infinitely variable type.

For this class the NBL/MAN L12V18/21S 12-cylinder engine was fitted with Napier turbochargers and was coupled to a six-pole main generator which provided current to the four traction motors. The generators and traction motors in the later locomotives were uprated to match the increased engine output. Like the WR units, they were carried on two four-wheel bogies, but the diesel-electric locomotives were fitted with a Commonwealth pattern

bogie of more orthodox appearance than the box-framed design fitted to the hydraulics. The class was numbered from D6100 upwards and became Class 29 in the 1968 renumbering scheme.

The 10 locomotives comprising the original order were delivered to the Eastern Region in 1959, where they joined two other classes in the Type 2 category. These were also new designs, being the first of the Birmingham/Sulzer (later Class 26) locomotives and the ill-starred English Electric 'Baby Deltics'.

All three types initially appeared on GN Line suburban and Cambridge services with varying degrees of unreliability. By the autumn of 1959 only two of the 10 NBLs were in use, the others having been returned to the makers or being under examination at Stratford. Meanwhile, the BRCW locomotives had also returned to their makers at Birmingham for attention. The ER allocated its Type 2s (D6100-37) to Hornsey, Stratford (for GE and LTS Line duties) and Ipswich but they rapidly gained an unenviable reputation for poor reliability. By early 1960 further diesel classes appeared on the ER, together with further deliveries of the successful Class 31 Brush A1A-A1As and two Type 1 designs. From the outset the performance of these classes was more encouraging and as deliveries of the Brush locomotives proceeded, so the NBL and BRCW types were transferred to the Scottish Region.

The first of the Scottish Region's own order for NBL Type 2s, No D6138, entered traffic in February 1960, and a month later the first 10 ER units were in store and sheeted over at Peterborough, awaiting removal to north of the Border. Kittybrewster received the first of these. By May pairs of the NBL locomotives transferred from the ER to Eastfield were at work on express passenger turns, and were noted on 'Bon Accord' and 'Granite City' Glasgow-Aberdeen

trains. Overall, the class was still showing itself less reliable than the BRCW locomotives which were by now in widespread use in Scotland. Problems with the NBL units continued in Scotland and in September 1960 no fewer than 21 were receiving attention at St Rollox, but by November they were beginning to take over some Glasgow-Dundee duties.

Crew training runs between Edinburgh Waverley and Dundee began in January 1961 and by April three pairs were employed on regular Glasgow-Dundee rosters. One such roster involved the 09.15 and 17.00 from Glasgow Buchanan Street and the corresponding 14.00 return trip from Dundee, finishing with an evening Dundee-Perth parcels working and a Perth-Glasgow passenger turn. On the Oban line they were set to work on the 00.12 Stirling-Oban, 06.05 Oban-Glasgow, 12.00 Glasgow-Oban and 17.15 return. A contemporary report remarked that they were not sparkling performers on the steep gradients of the Oban line, with significant understatement. Members of the class based at Eastfield were, at this time, finding employment on Glasgow-Carlisle freight services which arrived at Carlisle during the night. They returned on the 08.50 and 09.26 workings to Robroyston and the 18.03 to Buchanan Street.

Within weeks the NBL locomotives took over all Glasgow-Aberdeen passenger workings and had supposedly achieved a virtual monopoly of the express services from Buchanan Street. By July 1961, however, these workings returned to steam haulage on all but one return trip, and Dundee was obliged to borrow two 'A2' Pacifics to substitute for the troublesome diesels. On the GNS lines the majority of Aberdeen-Elgin through services then became diesel-hauled, and with the normal loading of four coaches and two or three vans the Type 2s had power to spare. The increased loadings of summer Saturday trains on this route severely taxed them, though, and

performance suffered accordingly. By the beginning of winter their workings on the Oban line declined and they returned to the Glasgow-Aberdeen duties, but after 1962 ex-LNER Pacifics predominated. Motive power staff had evidently encountered protracted difficulties in settling the class reliably into any of these rosters, in marked contrast to the way in which the BRCW and Brush Type 2s and even the humble EE Type 1s had found favour with their operators.

During the early 1960s various tests were carried out with members of the class, including some runs with No D6112 between Ayr Harbour and Dalmellington. These tests involved the operation of a train of more than 50 loaded mineral wagons over the steeply graded Dalmellington branch, a diesel brake tender being provided next to the locomotive. Eventually, operating staffs achieved a measure of reliability and the class made widespread, if somewhat erratic, appearances on most Scottish routes. In 1963 a Paxman Ventura engine was installed in D6123, and the new power unit, rated at 1,350hp, produced an encouraging improvement in performance. The refurbished locomotive, with an attractive two-tone green livery, was set to work on the Glasgow-Birmingham 'Condor' which was a vacuum brake fitted container train. With its 10ft wheelbase flat wagons and largely timber containers it seems remarkably antiquated by the standards of current Freightliner services.

The Glasgow-Aberdeen services again became a proving ground for the class and from September 1963 the Paxman-engined locomotive took over a diagram involving the 3hr 7.10 from Aberdeen and the 17.30 return. This duty had been the preserve of a Ferryhill 'A4' Pacific, and it is a measure of the improved reliability of the re-engined diesel that it soon became a regular performer on this turn. Nos D6103/6 were next to be converted, but by mid-1964 the availability of the original locomotives was so bad that a question mark hung over their future only four or five years after many of them had entered traffic. Deliveries of the curious centre-cab Clayton Type 1s had begun and these were put into traffic with enthusiasm while 12 of the NBLs lay stored at Parkhead steam depot and were gutted of engines and generators. No one could have guessed that many of the new Claytons would end their careers with pyrotechnic displays in even fewer years than the NBLs. The axe hung briefly over the stored locomotives before those empty hulks which had not been accident damaged were re-engined and refurbished. Nos D6101/2/14/6/21/30/3 were the next to be dealt with, followed by D6100/7/8/12/13/19/24/29/32/7 which brought the final tally of rebuilt machines to 20. By this time an obvious external alteration to many of the class had also occurred with the fitting of four-character headcode panels. Unlike

the WR units in which a pair of displays was placed either side of the gangway connection, the Scottish Region acknowledged that the gangways were seldom used, removed them, and placed the four-character display centrally on each end. A few of the later conversions were repainted in BR blue, and a number possessed to the end a 'T' shaped recess in the cab side where automatic tablet catchers had been fitted and later removed.

Although the Paxman units proved more reliable and the all-round performance of the locomotives was greatly improved, the conversions really came too late to affect their ultimate fate. By the late 1960s the re-engined examples had also taken up duties on other ScR lines such as the West Highland line where they were reasonably proficient and where they worked singly. Withdrawals began in 1967 concurrent with their WR diesel-hydraulic sisters and naturally all the original NBL/MAN engined survivors were early victims. The Paxmans remained safe until 1969 when

D6108 was the first to go, followed by the bulk of the class in 1970, leaving D6112/6/9/33 to soldier on until the end of 1971.

Sadly, none of the NBL main line diesels has been preserved to remind us of an unhappy and belated move to diesel traction by their builders, although two examples, one of the original 'Warships' and D6122 of the Type 2s, linger at Barry as vandalised hulks.

Left: One of the original Scottish Region allocation, No D 6149, awaits the right-away from Tillynaught Junction with the 14.10 Aberdeen-Inverness on 5 July 1963. / W. G. Sumner

Above: A Class 29 powered by a Paxman Ventura engine on their most prestigious duty, one of the Aberdeen-Glasgow 3hr trains. The train is between Gleneagles and Blackford on 7 July 1966. / John M. Boyes

Below: No 6130 had not much longer to live when on 22 August 1970 it headed a Glasgow (Queen St)-Dunfermline football special across the Forth Bridge. / G. J. Jackson

Patagonian steam to Esquel

H. R. STONES

From the southern boundary of Argentina's broad gauge railway network some 962 miles south-west of Buenos Aires, an interesting self-contained 2ft 5½in narrow gauge line operated by steam runs from Ingeniero Jacobacci in the province of Rio Negro to the small frontier town of Esquel in the remote southern province of Chubut close to the Alerces National Park and Lake District at the foot of the Andes.

This single-track line, 250 miles long and part of the South-West Region of the Argentine Railways, crosses the typically sun-baked, barren, undulating area of Patagonia and follows the contours of the Andean foothills with their deep canyons and valleys, through which flow rivers or streams for most or part of the year. In many places gradients are steep and curves sharp, for the railway was constructed economically to avoid as many large earthworks as possible. Many rivers are bridged, including the 500-mile long River Chubut on its way to the South Atlantic. The canyon valleys, sheltered from the fierce prevailing winds, are green with vegetation and in these localities sheep rearing is the major occupation. Much of the considerable wool production is transported north by rail to the manufacturing regions of the central provinces, and for export; other important traffics carried by the railway are alfalfa and hay.

The construction of the line to Esquel, which commenced in the early 1930s but was not completed throughout until 1950, was part of an overall plan by the Argentine Government in 1921 to extend railway communications south of the River Negro. This would, they hoped, open up and increase agricultural activities and sheep rearing in the region and promote tourism in the various picturesque lake districts close to the Southern Andes.

The first new railway comprised a broad gauge (5ft 6in) line, 392 miles long, from Puerto San Antonio on the Atlantic coast due west to San Carlos de Bariloche — gateway to the newly created National Park and the Lake District of Nahuel Huapi. Construction commenced in 1922, but due to financial and other difficulties the line did not reach San Carlos de Bariloche until 1934. In the meantime, in 1928, another section of broad gauge line had been completed from Puerto San Antonio east to Viedma on the River Negro. During the same year the river was bridged to provide a physical rail connection with the former British-owned broad gauge Buenos Aires Great Southern Railway at Carmen de Patagones on the opposite bank. As the result of this direct link with the main railway network to the north, it was decided to proceed with the construction of the railway to Esquel from Ingeniero Jacobacci which had already been reached by the broad gauge line still under construction to San Carlos de Bariloche. For reasons of economy the Esquel line was built to a gauge of 2ft 5½in which necessitated the transhipment of passengers and freight to and from the broad gauge system at Ingeniero Jacobacci. A previous project to connect Esquel with the now dismantled Chubut Central Railway, which served Puerto Madryn on the

South Atlantic coast, was abandoned.

At Ingeniero Jacobacci the narrow gauge passenger trains are served by a bay platform at the west end of the station, the line to Esquel running over the broad gauge line to San Carlos de Bariloche by means of a third rail for about 10 miles and then swinging away on its own to the south-west. For the first 50 miles the country is flat scrubland with stopping points (some conditional) at Ojos de Agua (27 miles), Futa Ruin (38 miles) and Manuel Choiqué (52 miles). From this point the line commences to rise sharply over the first group of foothills to Aguada Troncoso (66 miles) and Cerro Mesa (79 miles) — a veritable green oasis in barren surroundings. Continuing, the parched flat landscape unfolds endlessly as far as Fitalancao (108 miles) and after following a zig-zag route along the slopes of the canyon valleys, the line reaches Norquincó (125 miles) the half-way point on the railway. Over the next 20 miles the line drops down into the valley of the River Chubut, crossing this river shortly before reaching El Maitén (147 miles) just inside the province of Chubut. Here are located the repair shops and principal locomotive depot of the railway, where engines are changed, train crews relieved, and trains crossed to schedule. Also, the dining car on the tri-weekly up passenger train from Ingeneiro Jacobacci is detached and coupled up to the down train for the return working. From El Maitén the line continues along the west side of the valley with stations at Ingeniero J. Thomas (163 miles), Leleque (178 miles) and rises approaching Lepa (193 miles) to cross another group of foothills. Passing stations at Mayoco (208 miles) and La Cancha (220 miles), the line runs along a precarious ledge of the mountainside for several miles to finally gain access through a narrow gorge down to the Esquel Valley and to the terminus of the railway at Esquel (250 miles). This small but important frontier town, situated 1,212 miles by rail from Buenos Aires, is also the administrative centre for the extensive agricultural region to the south known as the '16th of October Colony'.

The Esquel line has been operated entirely by steam since it was opened, the motive power being provided

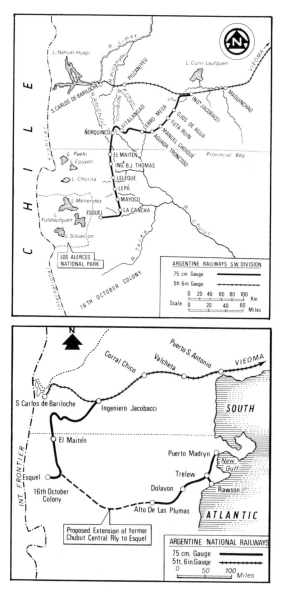

Above left: The parched, bleak landscape at Fitalancao is enlivened by Henschel 2-8-2 No 107 on a southbound passenger train. / Ken Mills

Below: Its train laden with wool and general freight, Baldwin 2-8-2 No 22 makes its way through desolation near Fitalancao. / Ken Mills

exclusively by two-cylinder oil-fired mixed-traffic 2-8-2 locomotives supplied in 1922 by Baldwin and Henschel. The original order placed by the Argentine Government comprised 25 locomotives (Class '75B') from Baldwin and 50 (Class '75H') from Henschel for use primarily at that time on the extension of the Chubut Central Railway (leased to the government in 1922 and converted to 2ft 5½in gauge) and, later, on the Esquel line when completed. Of the original 75 identical locomotives there are only 37 left, due mainly to cannibalisation over the years, and these are now all operating on the Esquel line. At El Maitén, the main locomotive depot, 27 are shedded while the remainder are allocated to sub-sheds at Ingeniero Jacobacci (six), Cerro Mesa (two) and Esquel (two). They are all provided with four-wheel bogie tenders and equipped with powerful electric headlights and cowcatchers. Principal dimensions are as follows below.

There is also a 0-6-0 side tank allocated to El Maitén for shunting the repair shops, this being one of two similar locomotives built by Henschel of Germany in 1922 (Works Nos 19452/19453).

The bogie passenger rolling stock includes a number of vehicles of the same vintage as the locomotives, having been built by the Ateliers Familleureux of Belgium in 1922. Both first and second class coaches are of the open saloon type with centre gangway, the former being equipped with a coal-fired stove at one end to provide heating during the long and severe Patagonian winters. Another interesting feature concerns the narrow gauge dining cars attached to passenger trains between Ingeniero Jacobacci and El Maitén. These have small tables with six single seats on either side of the centre gangway, meals being served from a miniature kitchen with a coal stove. Bogie freight vehicles include covered wagons for general merchandise and livestock and open wagons for bales of wool and hay. All locomotives and rolling stock are provided with centre couplings and continuous vacuum brake equipment.

Passenger or mixed trains are operated three times a week on Tuesday, Thursday and Saturday, connecting at Ingeniero Jacobacci with the broad gauge sleeping car expresses between Buenos Aires (Plaza Constitucion) and San Carlos de Bariloche. The up train leaves Ingeniero Jacobacci at 05.30 while the down train from Esquel arrives at 00.30, the overall journey occupying 15hr 35min and 15hr respectively, at an average speed of about 17mile/h in either direction. Apart from the passenger service there is a limited schedule of freight trains and on Monday, Wednesday and Friday a passenger coach is attached to the morning freight from both Ingeniero Jacobacci and Esquel. Passing loops, and locomotive fuel oil and watering points are suitably located at a number of intermediate stations.

Although dieselisation of the Esquel line has been under study in the past, in view of the cost involved

Class	Type	Nos	Cylinders (2) Dia (in)	Stroke (in)	Coupled wheels Dia (ft in)	Working pressure (lb/sq in)	Tractive effort at 80% working pressure (lb)	Builders	Works Nos
'75B'	2-8-2	1-25	12	17	2 7½	170	10,440	Baldwin (1922)	55429-55453
'75H'	2-8-2	101-150	12	17	2 7½	170	10,440	Henschel (1922)	19402-19451

Below left: Henschel 2-8-2 No 107 waits at El Maitén to haul southbound passenger train to Esquel.

Above: Looking smarter than most of its compatriots, Baldwin 2-8-2 No 115 has just been overhauled and repainted at the El Maitén workshops. / *Ken Mills*

Right: The El Maitén works pilot, a 1922-built Henschel 0- 6-0T. / *Ken Mills*

Below: The more hospitable surroundings of Esquel are being left behind by Henschel 2-8-2 No 104 climbing out of the frontier town with a northbound train of hay and wool. / *Ken Mills*

and severe winter weather in the area, it has been decided to retain the steam locomotives which are considered more suitable for the track gauge and local working conditions.

In conclusion, the writer wishes to acknowledge the invaluable assistance of Ken Mills, co-author of *World of South American Steam*, in the preparation of this article and for permission to reproduce his photographs.

The Chesham branch

FRANK W. GOUDIE

The Metropolitan Line branch from Chalfont to Chesham has an interesting history; although not originally on the route of the Metropolitan Railway's Northern Extension, Chesham was in fact the terminus of that line for three years. After Sir Edward Watkin became Chairman of the Metropolitan in 1872 the company, whose line from Baker Street had reached Swiss Cottage, began to develop main line aspirations. Watkin had grandiose plans for the Metropolitan, though he did not share his projects with subordinates, and even John Bell, the company's secretary, said that Watkin 'did not confide his policy to many people'. The Metropolitan metals were pushing north-westwards, but few seemed to know the ultimate objective.

A bill promoted by the company in 1889 empowered the Metropolitan to work over the Aylesbury & Buckingham Railway (Aylesbury to Verney Junction). Authority for the extension from Rickmansworth to Aylesbury had already been granted. Another bill, not in the Metropolitan's name, was for the Worcester & Broom Railway extension to Aylesbury. This would have authorised a connection with the East & West Junction Railway, which ran from Broom to Towcester, and would end by a connection with the Aylesbury & Buckingham. A junction with the Banbury branch of the LNWR was also envisaged. Together, the bills would have given the Metropolitan a through route to Worcester, the objective apparently being Birmingham, but the whole complicated scheme fell through, probably to the relief of the company's shareholders, who doubtless felt that Sir Edward was rather over-reaching himself. The Aylesbury & Buckingham Railway was, however, vested in the Metropolitan in 1890.

By 1887, the Metropolitan's tracks had penetrated as far into rural Hertfordshire as Rickmansworth. The extension of the line beyond this point was authorised by the Aylesbury & Rickmansworth Railway Act of 1881, and the contractor for building this section was, a Mr J. T. Firbank. Chesham was not originally included in the line's route but a deputation of Chesham residents who met the Metropolitan directors on 1 August 1884 complained that the company's proposed new station at the top of Rectory Hill, Amersham, would be three miles away from Chesham and very inconvenient. Sir Edward Watkin rejoined that the only remedy would be a branch line to Chesham. Subject to the approval of the directors, if a line could be projected which could ultimately be continued to the LNWR system at Tring (or allow the North Western to come down to Chesham), the Metropolitan would give notice for the necessary powers in the next session of Parliament. These powers were granted, but the connection with the LNWR at Tring never materialised — perhaps this time Watkin had cast his eyes on Birmingham again via North Western metals!

Below left: A through train from Baker Street-Chesham, some time before 1892, headed by Metropolitan 'A' class 4-4-0T No 9, formerly *Minerva*. / *Locomotive & General Railway Photographs*

Above: In the last months before the Metropolitan was absorbed into the LPTB, 'E' 0-4-4T No 1 brings the branch train of two 'Dreadnought' coaches into Chalfont station on 22 April 1933. / *H. C. Casserley*

Below: One of the Met's handsome 4-4-4Ts, No 103, brings a through train into Chesham on 22 April 1933. Right is stock for a Marylebone train with LNER 'A5' 4-6-2T No 5411 at its head. / *H. C. Casserley*

A Board meeting on 12 October 1887 resolved that the line from Rickmansworth to the junction at Amersham (the present Chalfont station) should be double track, with a single line branch to Chesham, plainly showing that the real objective was the extension to Aylesbury, with the Chesham line only an afterthought. Originally, the station at Chesham was to have been in Mill Field, about half a mile from the town centre, but the obvious inconvenience of this site led a committee of prominent Chesham citizens to be formed, headed by Mr W. Lowndes, who offered to purchase the land and property required for an extension of the line, parallel with the High Street, to a terminus at the north end of the town. Their offer was accepted by the Metropolitan, the committee raising £2,000 for the necessary land, which they then presented to the railway company.

Construction of the extension from Rickmansworth went ahead. In the meantime, in response to requests from Chesham residents, John Bell, the Metropolitan secretary, arranged with a Mr Large of the 'Swan Hotel' at Rickmansworth for a two-horse omnibus service between the 'Crown' at Chesham and Rickmansworth. Mr Large horsed and worked the service with a vehicle provided by the railway company (probably one of the buses which the Metropolitan was at that time operating in London). By July 1889 the line was ready for inspection by Major-General Hutchinson of the Board of Trade.

Hutchinson's report stated that the extension was 8 miles 16 chains in length, consisting of double track 4 miles 40 chains from Rickmansworth to Chalfont Road, with single track 3 miles 56 chains from that

latter part of last week the town crier made an announcement to the effect that the committee would be glad if the inhabitants would endeavour to decorate their residences, etc, on the day of the opening of the new railway', but commented that this occasion 'would long be remembered for the conspicuous absence of demonstrative effect'.

Even so, the event does not seem to have passed by unmarked, for the same newspaper reported that:

'across the Broadway, near the approach road to the station, was a streamer with the words "Forward be our watchword" on one side, and on the other "Our town, trade and industries". At the top of the road to the station was a similar streamer, displaying on the side facing the High Street "The long-looked-for come at last" and, on the other side, "Success to the Metropolitan Railway". At the station was hoisted the Company's flag.'

point to Chesham. The steepest gradient on the double track section was 1 in 100, with 1 in 66 on the Chalfont Road to Chesham line. Thirteen overbridges and 19 underbridges were involved, including a bridge of 30ft 6in span over the River Chess at Chesham. Signalboxes were built at the intermediate stations (Chorley Wood and Chalfont Road) and at Chesham, where there was also an engine turntable. General Hutchinson's report recommended various alterations to the signalling arrangements, and stipulated that the engineer must take steps to reduce the deflection in the girders of the bridge over the River Chess. Subject to these conditions being met without unnecessary loss of time, and the line presented for re-inspection, the Board of Trade would sanction its opening.

In fact, there were two opening ceremonies. The first was informal, when the line was inspected by Baron Ferdinand de Rochschild and the Metropolitan directors on 15 May 1889. A special through train was run, leaving Baker Street at 11.45 and arriving in Chesham at 13.10. The public opening took place on 8 July. The *Bucks Herald* reported that 'during the

The public dinner so customary at Victorian railway openings seems to have been absent; the bells of St Mary's Church were rung, but the brass bands were conspicuous by their silence. However, a large number of people assembled to see the departure of the first train at 06.55 and throughout the day the slope above the station was lined with spectators. About 1,500 passengers used the line on the opening day, and on the following day an excursion was run to the Crystal Palace.

After this the line seems to have settled down to its normal routine. The original train service consisted of through trains to Baker Street. Passengers for Inner Circle stations had to change at Baker Street until 1909, when track modifications at that station permitted through working from the Northern Extension Line. On 1 September 1892 the line from Chalfont Road to Aylesbury was opened, the same date seeing the start of a shuttle service from Chalfont Road to Chesham. On 2 April 1906 the Metropolitan

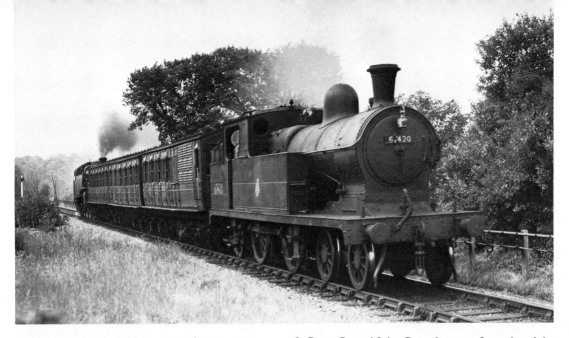

Above left: The Met's 0-6-4Ts, classified 'M2' by the LNER, were uncommon on passenger trains. On 27 May 1939, No 6157 (Met No 97 *Brill*) stands at the head of a through train in Chesham station. / *H. C. Casserley*

Below left: The familiar post-war Chesham branch combination of an ex-GCR 'C13' 4-4-2T and one of the Ashbury-built three-coach push-pull sets. No 7418 at Chalfont on 16 July 1948. / *F. W. Goudie*

Above: An unusual working on Saturday, 1 June 1957: BR '4' 2-6-4T No 80137 seems to be steaming hard at the rear of a Chesham push-pull soon after leaving the branch terminus. 'C13' No 67420 is at the front.
/ *E. R. Wethersett/Ian Allan Library*

Below: On the penultimate day of steam working on the Chesham shuttle, and with the conductor rails clearly apparent, Ivatt '2' 2-6-2T No 41284 stands in the main platform at Chesham on 10 September 1960. Note the bay platform (left). / *F. W. Goudie*

& Great Central Joint Committee was formed, and the Metropolitan lines north of Harrow came under its management; from this date some Great Central trains from Marylebone ran through to Chesham. From 1910 onwards Chesham branch passengers enjoyed the unusual luxury of a Pullman service when Pullman cars *Mayflower* and *Galatea* were included in certain through trains to Liverpool Street and Aldgate, a facility which continued until soon after the outbreak of World War II.

The next notable event to affect the line was the absorption of the Metropolitan by the London Passenger Transport Board on 1 July 1933, although, at first, this brought few changes in the working of the branch. On 1 November 1937 however, the LPTB handed over all steam working beyond Rickmansworth to the LNER, and that company's locomotives now hauled Metropolitan coaches between Rickmansworth, Aylesbury and Chesham, including the

Chesham shuttle service. Nationalisation initially had little effect on Chesham branch services, which continued to be worked by Eastern Region steam locomotives from Neasden shed.

Electrification of the Metropolitan Line from Rickmansworth to Amersham was announced in 1934, but work was suspended with the outbreak of war. In 1955 the prewar plans were modified, and the Chesham branch was included in the electrification scheme and as from 12 September 1960 electric services were extended beyond Rickmansworth to Amersham and Chesham.

Over the years the Chesham service has been worked by a variety of locomotive types. The earliest trains were worked by the well-known 'A' and 'B' class Beyer Peacock 4-4-0Ts. Later, the branch shuttle trains were formed of two compartment coaches of the 'Dreadnought' type, hauled by the Met's 'E' class 0-4-4Ts. Through trains from Baker Street and the City were graced by the handsome 'H' class 4-4-4Ts while the Marylebone trains were in the hands of ex-GCR 'A5' 4-6-2Ts.

After LT handed over the working of Metropolitan Line steam trains in 1937, and Neasden shed took on these duties, 'N5' 0-6-2Ts appeared on the branch shuttle with its two 'Dreadnought' coaches. But this entailed the engine running round at both Chesham and Chalfont, an inconvenient arrangement at the latter station thanks to the track layout. So, in 1940, LT converted some former electric multiple unit Ashbury-built compartment stock, from the turn of the century, to provide two three-coach sets for push-and-pull working on the Chesham branch. Originally built as steam stock, the coaches were converted for electric traction from 1905 onwards; when altered for the Chesham shuttle the former motor coaches had the control equipment compartments converted to guard's and luggage accommodation. The former driving trailers had the driver's compartments fitted with controls for steam push-and-pull working. Each three-coach train spent a week in service on the branch, and was changed over early on Sunday mornings, being worked from Neasden behind a Metropolitan electric locomotive to Rickmansworth, where it was handed over to the Chesham branch engine.

After World War II the Chesham branch duties were taken over by ex-GCR 'C13' 4-4-2Ts (the most familiar of which were Nos 67416/8/20), though for a short period in 1951 'N7' 0-6-2Ts made an appearance. The 'C13s' were eventually displaced by Ivatt Class '2' 2-6-2Ts which continued to handle the push-pull service until the branch was electrified in 1960. Incidentally, there was a proposal in 1936 for diesel railcars to work the shuttle, but this was not acted upon, and, of course, the postwar plans included the Chesham line in the electrification scheme.

After the 1960 electrification from Rickmansworth to Amersham and Chesham, the Chesham branch service was at first provided by a three-coach train of Metropolitan 'T' class compartment stock, supplemented by the Metrovick electric locomotives on through trains of steam stock from Baker Street

and the City. Towards the end of 1961 the Metropolitan stock was superseded by new 'A60' multiple units and these monopolise all workings today. An interesting working occurred on 22 May 1955 when the branch enjoyed a visit from the *Railway World* 'Metropolitan Special' consisting of ex-Metropolitan 0-4-4T No L44 and five 'Dreadnought' coaches, which included Chesham in its wider itinerary.

Information regarding goods trains to Chesham is rather scanty, but the Metropolitan working timetable for 1917 shows one goods train on the branch, Monday to Friday, arriving at Chesham at 02.40 and departing at 16.20, and the 1927 WTT shows a very similar service.

The bay platform at Chalfont for the Chesham line is on the up side, and at the northern end of the station. The line runs parallel with the Amersham line for about half a mile, then curves away northwards, past houses and a factory on the right, and then through open fields and woodland. Then begins the descent to Chesham, first through a deep cutting and then into open country, with a fine view of the Chess Valley on the right. Approaching Chesham much new housing development is passed before the line crosses the bridge over the River Chess and comes into Chesham station, a brick building in the rather undistinguished style used by the Metropolitan on the

Aylesbury line. Chesham now has only one platform face and track, though prior to electrification a run-round loop was provided, which has now been lifted. Just before electric services commenced a bay platform and track were laid in on the south side, but this track has now been removed. Chesham once boasted a goods yard, but the site of this is now occupied, perhaps inevitably, by a car park.

It seems a far cry from the early years of the Chesham branch, with, first, its Beyer Peacock 4-4-0Ts and, then, the Pullman cars, to the present day, with colour-light signalling and aluminium-bodied multiple unit electric trains. But, in many ways, it still has the atmosphere of a country branch line, even though many will regret the passing of the Metropolitan Railway's pleasing dark red locomotives and varnished teak carriages.

Above left: On 13 September 1960 the Chesham branch train is an electric multiple unit. 'T' stock motor car No 2735 of 1930 leads at Chalfont. / *F. W. Goudie*

Below left: Through trains brought the Metropolitan electric locomotives on to the Chesham branch. No 5 *John Hampden* (now preserved) at Chesham on 13 September 1960. / *F. W. Goudie*

Below: Chesham station in 1976. A train of A60 stock waits for custom. / *J. G. Glover*